An EEG-Based Brainwave Signature System for Biometric Authentication

A.ELAKKIYA

TABLE OF CONTENTS

FEATURE EXTRACTION AND CLASSIFICATION

LIST OF TABLES

BIT TRANSFER RATE

LIST OF ABBREVATIONS

SYMBOLS	ABBREVIATIONS
10-20	System 10%-20% International Electrode Placement System
A/D	Analog-to-Digital
AC	Alternating Current
AFIS	Automated Fingerprint Identification Systems
AP	Action Potentials
AR	Auto-Regressive
ARMA	Autoregressive-Moving-Average
ARMAX	Autoregressive Moving Average Exogenous
ATM	Automated Teller Machine
BCI	Brain-Computer Interface
BMI	Brain Machine Interface
C	Central
CASIA	Chinese Academy of Sciences Institute of Automation
CNS	Central Nervous System
CRT	Cathode Ray Tube
CSP	Common Spatial Patterns
Cz	Central Zone
DA	Discriminant Analysis
DBHT	Descriptor Based Hough Transform
DFT	Discrete Fourier Transform
DNA	Deoxyribonucleic Acid
DWFNNT	Discrete Wavelet Formants Neural Network
DWT	Discrete Wavelet Transform
DWTHRS	Discrete Wavelet Transform based Human Recognition System
ECG	Electrocardiogram
ECGI	Electrocardiogram Identification
ECoG	Electrocorticogram
EEG	Electroencephalogram

EER	Equal Error Rate
EMG	Electromyography
F	Refer to Frontal
FAR	False Acceptance Rate
FFBNN	Feed Forward Back Propagation Neural Network
FFT	Fast Fourier Transform
FIRDA	Frontal Intermittent Rhythmic Delta
FLE	Frontal Lobe Epilepsy
fMRI	Functional Magnetic Resonance Imaging
FPz	Frontal Polar Zone
FRR	False Rejection Rate
FT	Fourier Transform
FTA	Failure to Accept
FTE	Failure to Enroll
Fz	Frontal Zone
GBSP	Gamma Band Spectral Power
GMM	Gaussian Mixture Model
GUI	Graphical User Interface
HCI	Human Computer Interaction
Hz	Hertz
IBIA	International Biometric Industry Association
ICA	Independent Component Analysis
IWTHR	Integer Wavelet Transform based Human Recognition System
LD	Linear Discriminant
LVQ	Learning Vector Quantization
MA	Maximum A Posteriori Model Adaptation
MAP	Maximum A Posteriori
MATLAB	Matrix Laboratory
MCC	Minutia Cylinder Code
MCN	Modified combinatorial nomenclature
MFCC	Mel Frequency Cestrum Coefficients

MRI	Magnetic Resonance Imaging
mV	Millivolt
N	Number of samples
NEG	Negative
O	Occipital
OIRDA	Occipital Intermittent Rhythmic Delta
Oz	Occipital Zone
P	Parietal
BURG	Power Spectral Density Algorithm Using Burg
PCA	Principal Component Analysis
COV	Covariance
PCG	Phonocardiogram
MCOV	Modified Covariance
MUSIC	Multiple classification Algorithm
PDA	Personal Digital Assistant
PET	Positron Emission Tomography
PIN	Personal Identification Number
PNS	Peripheral Nervous System
POS	Positive
PSD	Power Spectral Density
Pz	Parietal Zone
RBF	Radial Basis Function
RBFNN	Radial Basis Function Neural Network
RNN	Recurrent Neural Network
ROC	Receiver Operating Curve
ROI	Region of Interest
RR	Recognition Rate
SFA	Simplified Fuzzy ARTMAP
SI	Speaker Identification
SNR	Signal to Noise Ratio
STFT	Short Time Fourier Transform

SVM	Support Vector Machine
SVMs	Support Vector Machines
T	Temporal
T	Time
TAR	True Acceptance Rate
VEP	Visual Evoked Potentials
VQ	Vector Quantization
WPT	Wavelet Packet Transform
WT	Wavelet Transform

LIST OF SYMBOLS

SYMBOLS	ABBREVIATIONS
a(k)	Autoregressive
σ	Variance
τ	Time parameter
a(k)	Autoregressive
x(t)	Linear function
μV	Microvolts
ε	Insensitive Loss Function
E_p	Total Least Square Error of order P
σ^2	Error Variance
x(n)	Signal in Discrete Form
t	Time
f(k)	Fourier Transform
e(k)	Noise Input
e(n)	Unobserved Input Data

CHAPTER 1

INTRODUCTION

1.1 INTRODUCTION

Biometrics are known as the science and technology of measuring and analyzing biological data. Biometric systems are used in two different modes such as verification (authentication) and identification. Human physiological and behavioral characteristic can be used as a biometric characteristic as long as it satisfies the following requirements:

i.   **Uniqueness:** No two persons should have the same characteristic, and each relevant person should only have one original characteristic.

ii. **Universality:** This characteristic must exist in all individuals in the population being measured.

iii. **Permanence:** This characteristic should be time-invariant and must be a permanent part of the individual.

iv. **Authentication:** The characteristic must be able to match against similar characteristics and a positive or negative match must be able to made based on the measurement.

v.   **Collectability:** The characteristic can be measured. However, in a practical biometric system i.e., a system that employs biometrics for personal recognition.

In this research, a biometric authentication system using brain signature is developed and validated using experimental identification.

The term biometrics is derived from the Greek word bio (life) and metric (to measure) automated biometric system have only become available over the last few decades, due to significant advances in the field of computer processing, many of these new automated techniques, however, are based on ideas that were originally conceived hundreds, even thousand of year ago. Biometrics refers to the automatic recognition of individuals based on their physiological and behavioral characteristics. The biometric characteristics can be divided in two main classes:

1) Physiological are related to shape of the body. For examples fingerprint, face recognition, hand geometry, iris recognition and retina which has largely replaced retina, and odor/scent.
   a. Fingerprint: The analysis of an individual's unique fingerprints
   b. Face recognition: The analysis of the facial characteristics
   c. Hand geometry: The analysis of the shape of the hand and the length of the fingers
   d. Iris recognition: The analysis of the colored ring that surrounds the eye 's pupil
   e. Retina: The analysis of the capillary vessels located at the back of the eye.

2) Behavioral are related to behavior of a person. For examples typing rhythm, gait, and voice. Some researchers have coined the term behavioral metrics for this class of biometrics.
   a) Signature: The analysis of the way a person signs his name
   b) Vein: The analysis of pattern of veins in the back if the hand and the wrist
   c) Voice: The analysis of the tone, pitch, cadence and frequency of a person's voice.

A biometric system is essentially a pattern recognition system that recognizes an individual by comparing the binary code of a uniquely specific biological or physical characteristic to the binary code of the stored characteristic. Samples are taken from individuals to check if there is any similarity to biometric references previously taken from known individuals. The system then applies a specialized mathematical algorithm to the sample and converts it into a binary code and then compares it to the template sample to determine if the individual can be recognized. A reference model or reference containing the biometric properties of a person is stored in the system generally after data compression by recording their individual characteristics. These characteristics may be acquired several times during enrollment in order to get a reference profile that corresponds most with reality (Jain et al., 2004).

This measurable characteristic the biometric, can be primarily anatomical such as eye, face, finger image, hand, and voice or primary behavioral such as signature and typing rhythm, but most biometrics combine both anatomical and behavioral components. The biometric system must be able to identify a person based on one or a combination of these biometric identifiers quickly, automatically, and with little or no human intervention in the decision. They include the following:

A. Fingerprint Verification

B. Hand Geometry

C. Speaker Verification

D. Retinal Scanning

E. Iris Scanning

F. Facial Recognition

Biometrics is a very attractive technology, because it can be integrated into any application requiring security or access control, effectively eliminating risks associated with less advanced technologies. Iris recognition is extremely accurate, but expensive to implement and needs the cooperation of the person. Fingerprints are reliable and non-intrusive but not suitable for non-collaborative individuals (Jain et al., 2000). Some of the drawbacks of the existing biometric system are summarized below:

A. Fingerprint
1. Has rationally been associated with criminal activities and thus users could be reluctant to adopt this for biometric authentication
2. Social stigma such that it is related to literate
3. Variation occurs due to age, cut or due to working condition
4. Rare situations like people without fingers

B. Hand Geometry

1. Not unique to every user
2. Physical contact includes public hygiene
3. Not very distinctive
4. Mutation

C. Speaker Verification

1. Back ground noise must be controlled for accurate verification
2. Large storage space required
3. Easily influenced circumstances such as sore throat, common cold
4. Possibility of voice imitation
5. Possibility of crating nonexistent identities with text to speech technology
6. Possibility in rare case where voice is lost

D. Retina Scans

1. Extremely intrusive
2. Low user acceptance rate
3. Extremely expensive

E. Iris Recognition

1. Sampling the iris patterns requires much user cooperation or complex
2. Expensive input device
3. Iris authentication is hampered by vision aid
4. A lot of memory for the data to be stored

F. Facial Recognition

1. Data acquisition is difficult, user must face in same position each access, background lighting important for accurate verification
2. Face authentication requires images taken in a good controlled lighted environment
3. Disguise-a major obstacle
4. Usage may hamper due to social stigma

EEG as a biometric is relatively new compared to other biometrics. This modality has several advantages:

     i.   It is confidential (as it corresponds to a biometric tasks)

    ii.   It is difficult to mimic (as similar mental task are person dependent)

   iii.   It is almost impossible to steal (as brain activity is sensitive to the stress and the mood of the person to produce his / her mental pass-phrase).

1.2 BIOMETRIC SYSTEMS

A biometric system or a biometric device is a real-time system which recognizes a person by measuring a particular physical or behavioral characteristic and later comparing it to a library of characteristics belonging to one or many people (Ashbourn et al., 2003). The architecture of the system is dependent on whether it is used for verification and identification.

- **Verification:** In this mode, the system performs a one-to-one search, comparing the captured biometric data with the biometric templates stored in the system database. If a match is made the identity of the person is verified.

- **Identification**: This mode is used when the identity of the individual is not known in advance. The entire template database is then searched for a match to the individual concerned in a one-to-many search. If a match is made, the individual is identified.

1.2.1 Applications of Biometric Systems

The applications of biometrics can be divided into the following three main groups.

- **Commercial** applications include Computer Network Login, Electronic Data Security, E-Commerce, Internet Access, ATM, Credit Card, Physical Access Control, Cellular Phone, Medical Records Management, And Distance Learning.

- **Government** applications are Aadhaar - National ID Card, Correctional Facility, Driver's License, Social Security, Welfare Disbursement, Border Control, And Passport Control.
- **Forensic** applications such as Corpse Identification, Criminal Investigation, Terrorist Identification, Parenthood Determination and Missing Children (Daugman et al., 1999).

1.3 ELECTROENCEPHALOGRAM (EEG)

EEG records the electrical activity of the brain. EEG is a technique that reads scalp electrical activity generated by brain structures. Local current flows are formed when brain cells are activated. EEG measures in generally current flows during synaptic excitations of the dendrites of many pyramidal neurons in the cerebral cortex. Brain cells produce tiny electrical impulse that facilitates thought, memory and motion to communicate. The existence of electrical currents in the brain was discovered in 1875 by a Liverpool surgeon named Richard Caton 1842-1926. He studied action potentials from the exposed brains of rabbits and monkeys. Hans Berger 1873-1941, a German neuropsychiatrist. In 1924, he used his ordinary radio equipment to amplify the brain's electrical activity measured on the human scalp. Berger was the first to use the word "Electroencephalogram" to describe the brain electric potentials in humans. He placed the foundations for many of the present applications for EEG and as a result, which earned him the title as "Father of EEG" (Tudor et al., 2005).

1.4 PROBLEM STATEMENT

Many biometric techniques commercially available have many drawbacks as discussed which fail safe biometric. Biometric technology systems available today are not suitable for high security authentication system as they can be easily duplicated. The proposed biometric system using brain signatures is verified for its application in authentication system.

1.5 THESIS OBJECTIVES

This research has three main objectives namely,

1. To develop suitable protocols for EEG brain signal acquisition from biometric tasks.
2. To develop suitable feature extraction and classification algorithms for verifying individuals.
3. To design and development of a Graphical User Interface (GUI) for biometric verification from brain signature.

1.6 THESIS ORGANIZATION

The research work towards developing biometric authentication system using brain signature is presented with detail data acquisition of EEG signal, preprocessing, feature extraction, neural network and design a graphical user interface. The thesis is organized as follows.

Chapter 1 presents a brief overview of the research, such as introduction of biometrics, working principle, processing techniques and advantages and disadvantages of existing biometric techniques. EEG, problem statement, objective of thesis and thesis organization are also discussed here.

Chapter 2 discusses the review of literature which is a critical outlook at the existing research that is significant to the work carried out. This chapter briefly introduces the background knowledge and surrounding information about this research on the fundamentals of EEG, EEG rhythms, EEG based person authentication and identification, feature extraction and classification techniques. The work of several researchers are quoted and used as an evidence to support the concepts explained in this research work.

Chapter 3 explains the proposed methodology and various phases of research. The overall architecture is discussed here. This chapter elucidates EEG electrode placement, electrode type and data collection for single channel and two channel systems and preprocessing is done.

Chapter 4 discusses feature extraction techniques used in the proposed research, namely parametric, non-parametric and high resolution method. Basic artificial neural network and various designing parameters of neural network.

Chapter 5 tabulates, discusses and compares the classification and single trial analysis results obtained while testing the proposed system.

Chapter 6 concludes the proposed study. It also discusses the completion of proposed objectives and scope of future extension.

CHAPTER 2

LITERATURE REVIEW

2.1 INTRODUCTION

This chapter, discusses the background literature on the biometric, EEG characteristics, EEG, feature extraction and classification algorithms based on neural networks.

2.2 BIOMETRIC

Any biological or physiological signal like a fingerprint, retinal scan or speech matching (Paranjape et al., 2008) that can be used to identify a person (Jain et al. 2004) is called biometric. A biometric system is used for the recognition features, possessed by the person. Human behavior is an area of research in psychological studies (Jain et al., 1999) focused on understanding the conscious or unconscious reaction of the human being in relation to his environment. Behavior happens in time. Behavior is the basis for this research. When a trait is related to a dynamic action of the user, it is called as a behavioral biometric trait. Biometrics is the science of automatically identifying individuals based on their unique physiological or behavioral characteristics. These characteristics are also called biometric identifiers and they must be distinctive and measurable in order to identify individuals. Biometrics systems which are based on fingerprints, iris, palm print, retina, and face are widely used in diversity of area for user authentication; these approaches are gaining much popularity in the technology world. Unfortunately, they have caught with some abatement which degrades its performance (Woodward et al., 2003). One of the main differences between physical and behavioral biometric is the exploitation of the information, content across time in behavioral biometrics, as opposed to the commonly used instant acquisition in physical traits. There are two types of biometric systems that enable the link between a person and his / her identity includes verification and identification (Jain et al., 2004).

Discrete Wavelet Transform (DWT) with logarithmic Power Spectral Density (PSD) is combined for speaker formants extraction, to be used as evident classification features by (Daqrouq et al. 2009). For classification, Feed Forward Back Propagation Neural Network (FFBNN) method is proposed. The Discrete Wavelet Formants Neural Network (DWFNNT) system works with excellent capability of features tracking even with 0dB Signal-to-Noise Ratio (SNR).The results show excellent performance with 93.21% Recognition Rate (RR).

2.3 BIOLOGICAL MEASUREMENTS

Any biological measurement, analysis and many other factors contribute to the success or failure of the process. All of these factors fall into two general categories: properties of the characteristics measured and properties of the measurement process. So, any human physiological or behavioral characteristic can be used as a biometric characteristic as long as it satisfies the following requirements:

i. **Uniqueness:** No two persons should have the same characteristic, and each relevant person should only have one original characteristic.

ii. **Universality:** This characteristic must exist in all individuals in the population being measured.

iii. **Permanence:** This characteristic should be time-invariant and must be a permanent part of the individual.

iv. **Authentication:** The characteristic must be able to match against similar characteristics and a positive or negative match must be able to be made based on the measurement.

v. **Collectability:** The characteristic can be measured. However, in a practical biometric system, i.e., a system that employs biometrics for personal recognition, there are a number of other issues to be considered, including:

❖ **Performance:** Refers to the achievable recognition accuracy and speed, the resources required to achieve them, as well as the operational and environmental factors that affect the accuracy and speed.

❖ **Acceptability:** Indicates the extent to which people are willing to accept the use of a particular biometric characteristic in their daily lives.

❖ **Circumvention:** Reflects how easily the system can be fooled using fraudulent methods. The practical biometric system should meet the specified recognition accuracy, speed, and resource requirements, be harmless to the users, be accepted by the intended population, and be sufficiently robust to various fraudulent methods and attacks to the system (Jain et al., 2004).

2.4 BIOMETRIC MODALITIES

Biometric systems are divided on the basis of the authentication medium used. They are broadly divided as identifications technology as given:

- Fingerprints,
- Face Recognition,
- Palm Print
- Iris
- Voice Recognition.

2.4.1 Finger Print

Finger prints are the tiny ridges, whorls and valley patterns on the tip of each finger. Finger print recognition is one of the most adopted techniques for user identification. This is considered as a most reliable, feature and the cost of implementing finger print recognition method is very less than other biometric features. It is used in many forensic and commercial applications such as criminal investigation, electronic personal ID cards, etc. (Sravya et al., 2012). The finger print is the pattern of ridges and valleys on the tip of a finger and is used for personal verification of people. Fingerprint based recognition method is used because of its relatively outstanding features of universality, permanence, uniqueness, accuracy and low cost has made it most popular and a reliable technique and is currently the leading biometric technology (Jain et al., 2004).

Robust alignment algorithm is addressed to align fingerprints and measures similarity between fingerprints by considering both minutiae and orientation field information. Alignment between a latent and a rolled print is a difficult problem because latent often contain a small number of minutiae and undergo large skin distortion. Using these two problems, they proposed the Descriptor-Based Hough transform (DBHT), which is a combination of the generalized Hough transforming and a local minutiae descriptor, called Minutia Cylinder Code (MCC) (Alessandra et al., 2013). Automated Fingerprint Identification Systems (AFIS) which had played an important role in many forensics and civilian applications. The baseline matching algorithm took only minutiae as input and consists of the following steps: 1) Local minutiae matching 2) Global minutiae matching 3) Matching score computation. The minutiae-based baseline improved to extended features was used. A pair of fingerprints is classified by Support Vector Machine (SVM). Limitation of the proposed method is the poor quality of ridge impressions (Jain et al., 2014). The Gradient based approach was proposed by (Aggarwal et al., 2008) that capture textural information by dividing each minutiae neighborhood locations into several local regions of which histograms of oriented gradients are then computed to characterize textural information around each minutiae location. A texture feature of energy of a fingerprint can be used for effecting fingerprint verification (Jhat et al., 2011).

2.4.2 Face Recognition

Face recognition technique records face images through a digital video camera and analyses facial characteristics like the distance between eyes, nose, mouth, and jaw edges. These measurements are broken into facial planes and retained in a database, further used for comparison. Face recognition can be done in two ways such as face appearance and face geometry (Chellappa et al., 1995). Principal Component Analysis (PCA) is used, a feature extractor for face recognition by (Kirby et al., 1990). The main objective of the neural network in the face recognition is the feasibility of training a system to capture the complex class of face patterns. The neural networks are nonlinear in the network and so it is the widely used technique for face recognition. The authors achieved 96.2% accuracy in the face recognition process when using 400 images of 40 individuals.

The drawback of the neural network approach arises when the number of classes increases. (Karungaru et al., 2004) proposed template matching in which other face templates can be exploited from different prospects to characterize single face. The 188 images are extracted from 47 subjects. The pattern matching algorithm is a very practical approach, very simple to use and approximately achieves 100% recognition rate. The PCA using Eigen face provides the linear arrangement of templates. The complexity arises only during the extraction of the template.

2.4.3 Palm Print

A palm print refers to an image acquired from the palm region of the hand. The palm itself consists of principal lines, wrinkles and epidermal ridges and can be used for personal verification (Zhang et al., 2004). There are two types of palm print verification system namely high resolution and low resolution. Palm prints can be used for criminal, forensic, or commercial applications (Shu, 1998). The competitive coding scheme is used for palm print. This scheme extracts the orientation information from the palm lines and stores it in the competitive code. The proposed coding scheme has been evaluated using a database with 7,752 palm print images from 386 different palms. For verification, the proposed method can operate at a high genuine acceptance rate of 98.4% and a low false acceptance rate of 3*10-6 (Kong et al., 2011).

A novel algorithm for the automatic classification of low-resolution palm prints is experimented by (Huang et al., 2008). The local information about the extracted part of the principal line is used to decide a Region of Interest and then a suitable line detector is chosen to extract the next part of the principal line in this Region of Interest (ROI). The palm prints are classified into six categories considering the number of the principal lines and their intersections. From the statistical results in the database containing 13,800 palm prints, the proposed algorithm classified these palm print with 96.03% accuracy. This palm print authentication methods require that the input palm print should be matched against a large number of imprints in a database, which is very time consuming. A high resolution approach for palm print recognition with multiple feature extraction is done by (Dai et al., 2012). For orientation estimation the Discrete Fourier Transform (DFT) and radon-transform-based orientation estimation is used. For minutiae extraction, Gabor filter is used for ridges enhancement according to the local ridge direction and density. To extract the principal line features, Hough transform is applied. SVM is used as the fusion method for the verification system and the proposed heuristic rule for the identification system. However the proposed systems are based on encoding and matching creases, which are not as reliable as ridges.

2.4.4 Iris

The iris is a thin circular diaphragm, which lies between the cornea and the lens of the human eye, responsible for controlling the diameter and size of the pupil and thus the amount of light reaching the retina. The eye color is defined by the color of the iris. In optical terms, the pupil is the eye's aperture and the iris is the diaphragm that serves as the aperture stop (Flom et al., 1987). Iris biometrics system performance on a larger dataset based on the Gaussian Model constructed from a smaller data set. The database contains "non-ideal" iris images of 108 irises with 6 images per iris. They formed 54 vectors, each of size 6 and 108 vectors, each of size 3 samples of genuine. The distance between a pair of Iris subjects is defined as a K-dimensional Hamming Distance, modeled as Gaussian distribution. Database resulted in a reduction of the search space by an average of 84% at a 100% hit rate. The main factor for the amount of speedup during verification was the penetration rate of the indexing (Schmid et al., 2006).

Automated biometric iris recognition is where segmentation and matching process are implemented using Histogram Equalization and Gaussian smoothing filter. The experiment was performed with a sample of 67 grayscale images which were selected from the Chinese Academy of Sciences Institute of Automation (CASIA) database. Because of this, few pixel spaces between iris and pupil center, contour is wrongly segmented by the Hough transform. Subsequently, with adjusted parameters and Hough transform with SURF technique, satisfactory result was obtained. This system handles users falling into the Fail to Enroll (FTE) category (Sonia Sangwan et al., 2015). A biometric security technique for Integer

Wavelet Transform based Human Recognition System (IWTHRS) using iris images verification. Data set contains 756 gray scale eye images with 108 unique eyes or classes and 7 different images of each unique eye. The features of the normalized Iris are extracted using Integer Wavelet Transform and Discrete Wavelet Transform. The Hamming Distance is used for matching of two iris feature vectors. It is observed that the time required for feature extraction in case of IWTHRS is more when compared DWT based Human Recognition System (DWTHRS) (Prashanth et al., 2009). Iris encoding is generated from the inner product of the output from a 1D Log Gabor filter and secret pseudorandom numbers. In the segmentation stage, first an edge map is generated using a Canny edge detector. A Circular Hough Transform is used to obtain the iris boundaries. The isolated iris part is unwrapped into a rectangle with a resolution of 20 * 240 using Daugman's rubber sheet model. In matching, Hamming Distance is used to indicate the dissimilarity between a pair of iris codes. The sampling the iris patterns requires much users cooperation (Chin et al., 2006).

2.4.5 Voice Recognition

Our voice is influenced by the characteristics of the format of our body, by the physical constrains the body produces in the sound wave, and by the temporal characteristics derived from our cognitive processing and timing of sound producing. Inherent properties of the speaker like fundamental frequency, nasal tone, cadence, inflection, etc. are used for speech authentication (Hebert, 2008). GMM are used for authentication of speaker verification system. For each frame, a dimensional feature vector is extracted, the Discrete Fourier spectrum is obtained via a Fast Fourier transform from which magnitude squared spectrum is computed and put it through a bank of filters. The Mel-scale Cepstral Coefficients are computed from the outputs of the filter bank. GMM classifier is used. GMM-based density estimation achieves a significant recognition rates due to low FAR (False Acceptance rate) and FRR (False Rejection Rate). Possibility in rare case voice is lost (Mohamed Soltane et al., 2010). A hybrid scheme which appropriately incorporates the advantages of both the generative and discriminat model paradigms is described and evaluated by (Rafik Djemili et al., 2007). Support Vector Machines (SVMs) are trained to divide the whole speakers' space into small subsets of speakers within a hierarchical tree structure. During testing a speech token is assigned to its corresponding group and evaluation using Gaussian Mixture Models (GMMs) is then processed. A significant improvement compared to the baseline system is reported, a relative reduction in identification error rate up to 50% is reached, independently, neither on the training data size nor on the testing utterances lengths

2.5 BACKGROUND KNOWLEDGE RELATED TO ELECTROENCEPHALOGRAM

Electroencephalogram (EEG) is a record of the electrical activity of the brain and is a tool which gives an insight into the brain functions thereby helping the physicians to diagnose various abnormalities. Recording electrical oscillations of the brain began in 1875, when the British neurophysiologist Richard Caton first recorded the electrical activity of the brains of rabbits and monkeys directly from the brain tissue Caton 1875. The first human EEG was recorded in 1924 by Hans Berger, a German psychiatrist Berger 1929 (Collura, 1993). Since the days of Berger and the verification of his recordings by Jasper and Carmichael 1935, EEG has taken its place as a standard laboratory investigation in clinical neurophysiology and neurology. It is used in the diagnosis of brain pathology, e.g., epilepsy, sleep disorders and disorders of the nervous system. EEG recording is also used extensively in psychophysiological research and in the testing of drugs pharmacology Pryse-Phillips 1997. Already at that time, Berger noticed that brain waves varied with the individual's state of consciousness (Tyner, 1989).

During the EEG test by (Niedermeyer et al., 1993) a number of small discs called electrodes are placed to different locations on the surface of the scalp with temporary glues. Then each electrode is connected to an amplifier (one amplifier per pair of electrodes) and an EEG recording machine. The electrical signals from the brain are converted into wavy lines on a computer screen to record the results. EEG recordings, depending on their use, can have from 1 to 256 electrodes recorded in parallel, which is called multichannel EEG recordings. One pair of electrodes usually makes up a channel. Each channel produces a signal during an EEG recording.

There are two types of EEG depending on where the signal is taken in the head: scalp or intracranial. For the scalp EEG, small electrodes are placed on the scalp with good mechanical and electrical contact. Special electrodes implanted in the brain during the surgery result in intracranial EEG. On the other (Bronzino, 1995) the EEG measured directly from the cortical surface using subdural electrodes is called the Electrocardiogram (ECG). The amplitude of an EEG signal typically ranges from about 1 to 100 µV in a normal adult, and it is approximately 10 to 20 mV when measured with subdural electrodes such as needle electrodes. Since the architecture of the brain is non-uniform and the cortex is functionally organized, the EEG can vary depending on the location of the recording electrodes (David Millet et al., 2001).

2.6 EEG CHARACTERISTICS

EEG measures brain waves of different frequencies within the brain. EEG signals are sinusoidal waves, their amplitude is normally between 0.5 and 100 µV. After applying a Fourier Transform to the raw signals, the power spectrum is generated for four groups of waves. In general, EEG signals represent the combination of waveforms, and are generally classified according to their: Frequency, Amplitude (power), wave morphology (shape), spatial distribution topography and reactivity (behavioral state) (Bronzino et al., 1995).

2.7 FREQUENCY BANDS

The most familiar classification uses EEG waveform. These waveforms are essential tools for analyzing human brain activity. The raw EEG is usually described in terms of frequency bands are shown in Figure 2.1.

2.7.1 Delta Waves (Less than 4 Hz)

These are large amplitude waves, which occur in deep sleep and are associated with some abnormal processes and are said to reflect the unconscious mind. Delta waves are found in infants up to about one year of age and are present in stages 3 and 4 of sleep. These waves produce immobile, lethargic and less attentive states. Delta activity is usually most prominent frontally in adults and posteriorly in children (Nunez, 1995).

2.7.2 Theta Waves (4 Hz to 8 Hz)

Theta is also classed in the 'slow' category and occurs in connection with creativity, emotions, intuition and is associated with the subconscious mind. While theta waves are abnormal in awake adults, they are perfectly normal in children up to 13 years of age and in sleep. It is usually regional in spread, may involve many lobes, and can be lateralized or diffuse.

2.7.3 Alpha Waves (8 Hz to 13 Hz)

Alpha is a common state of the brain and occurs whenever a person is alert. It is a marker for alertness and sleep, but not actively processing information. Alpha has been linked to extroversion introverts show less, creativity subjects show alpha when listening and coming to a solution for creative problems and mental work. They are strongest over the occipital back of the head cortex and also over frontal cortex.

2.7.4 Beta Waves (13 Hz to 30 Hz)

These are low amplitude or 'fast' waves and are found during the waking state as well as when the brain is working as in some calculation or thinking process. It reflects desynchronized active brain tissue. It is usually seen on both sides of the cortex in symmetrical distribution and is most evident frontally. It may be absent or reduced in areas of cortical damage. Low beta activity 12-15 Hz is localized by side and by lobe and represents a relaxed yet alert state; Range beta 15-18 Hz is localized over several areas often associated with thinking and finally, High beta above 18 Hz corresponds to a strongly localized activity leading to agitated mental activity such as planning, math calculation etc. (Ridderinkhof et al., 2003).

2.7.5 Gamma Waves (36 Hz to 44 Hz)

This is the only frequency group distributed over every part of the brain. It is hypothesized and in some cases validated that the 40 Hz activity in the brain consolidates the required areas for simultaneous processing whenever the brains needs to access information from multiple regions. A good memory is associated with well-regulated and efficient 40 Hz activity, whereas a 40 Hz deficiency creates learning disabilities (Miltner et al., 1999).

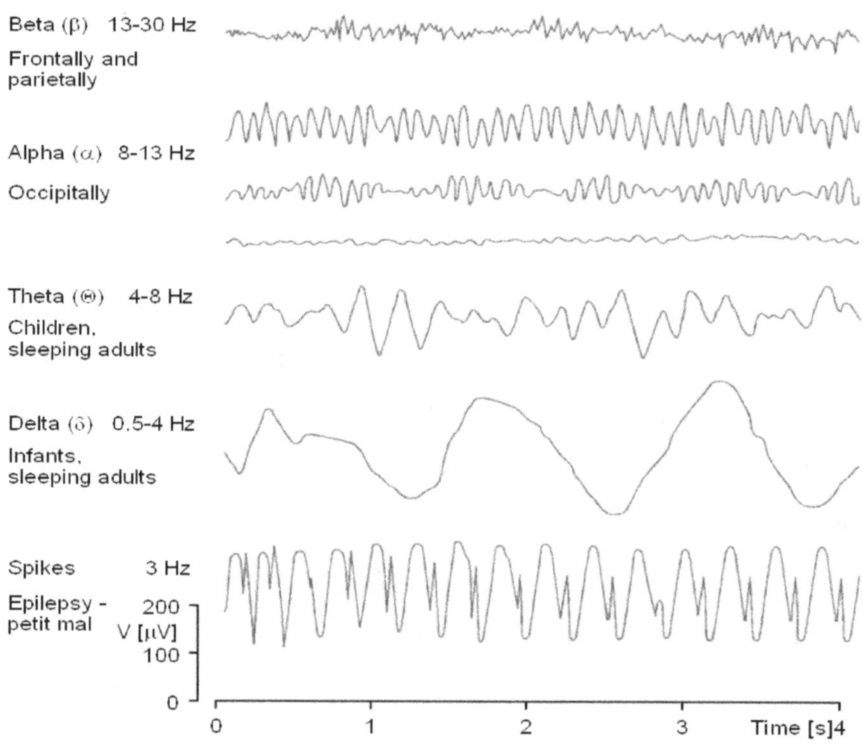

Figure 2.1 Different types of normal EEG rhythms (Lotte, 2009).

2.8 ELECTRODE PLACEMENT CONFIGURATIONS

Standardized electrode placement scheme known as the International 10-20 system (Jasper et al., 1958) was established, allowing the comparison of different EEG data derived from different subjects. This universal arrangement of electrodes known as the international ten twenty system, assures reproducible electrode sites with sufficient coverage of all parts of the head as depicted (Manzoor Khazi et al., 2012). The different electrode positions are derived from measurements taken between standard landmarks on the skull (Sabarigiri, 2014). These measurements allow the calculation of a network of lines, which are superimposed across the head. Electrodes are placed where the lines of this mesh intersect. This results in inter-electrode distances of ten and twenty percent of a line's total length. In this convention, each electrode site has a letter identifying its sub- cranial lobe i.e. Fp -Front polar or prefrontal lobe, 'F'-Frontal lobe, 'T'- Temporal lobe, 'C'-Central lobe, 'P'-Parietal lobe, 'O'-Occipital lobe. In addition, there is a number or another letter identifying its hemispherical location. The subscript 'Z' denoting line zero ensuing any lobe abbreviation refers to an electrode placed along the cerebrum's midline. The use of an even number 2, 4, 6 or 8 represents the right hemisphere and odd numbers 1, 3, 5 or 7 referring to the left hemisphere (Teplan, 2002).

The numbers rise with increasing distance from the midline of the head. The distances are calculated as percentages of typical lengths such as the head circumference etc. Percentages are made use of because the skull varies from subject to subject. An adolescent may be smaller than an adult and also traumatic accidents to the skull may have occurred in the subject's history creating an out of proportion condition (Schalk et al., 2004). The percentage relationship remains the same for the location of the internal brain lobes. Skull dimensions are measured accordingly in centimeters and then site distances or spacing are converted with the 10% and 20% factors. Fifty percent is used frequently, but is a composite of 10, 20 and 20%. Supplementary electrodes to those typically employed in the 10-20 system have been devised to improve electroencephalographic spatial resolution. This more extensive placement scheme using Modified Combinatorial Nomenclature (MCN) was developed by the American Clinical Neurophysiology Society and it broadens the 10-20 system by subdividing the existing inter- electrode distances as in the Figure 2.2 (Srinivasan et al., 1998).

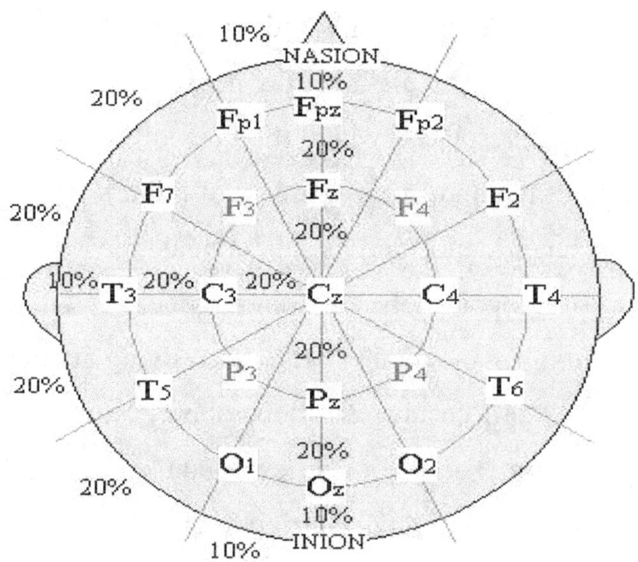

Figure 2.2 Standard Electrode Sites of The International 10-20 System

In recent times, the limited spatial resolution of the conventional EEG technology has been tackled by introducing High Resolution EEG HR- EEG (Babiloni et al., 1997; Edlinger et al., 1998). A pre-requisite for such methods is adequate sampling of the potential distribution on the scalp surface. The point-spread function of conduction of potential from the brain surface to the scalp averages about 2.5 cm (Gevins, 1990). Thus to adequately cover the surface of the scalp with electrodes having inter- electrode distance in this range, EEG equipment supporting at least 128 channels is required (Srinivasan et al., 1998). In accordance with this need, the state-of-the-art technology in EEG recording uses machines with up to 256 electrode positions.

2.9 SIGNAL ANALYSIS

Anything which carries some information is called a signal. However to derive useful information from the raw signal it demands a kind of standard way of representation. In order to represent a raw signal in a standard notation, the signal has to undergo a series of operation. The serious operation together is called as "signal processing". There are three basic ways in which the signals are analyzed by (Blanco et al., 1995). There are Time Domain analysis, Frequency Domain analysis and Time and Frequency Domain analysis.

2.10 EEG-BASED PERSON AUTHENTICATION AND IDENTIFICATION

Person identification and person authentication are two different types of applications and thus pose different challenges on decision making of biometric systems. The goal of person identification is to identify an individual from a group of persons, i.e. matching the biometric features of one person against all the records in a database, while the goal of person authentication is to confirm or deny an identity claim by a particular individual. We are particularly interested in person authentication in this thesis. An authentication and identification system often consists of two main components, they are EEG feature extraction and pattern identification.

A two-stage threshold method to verify 5 subjects was proposed by (Palaniappan et al.,2008) based on the features of Autoregressive Coefficients (AR), channel spectral powers and Inter-Hemispheric Channel Spectral Power Differences (IHPD), Inter-Hemispheric Channel Linear Complexity (IHLC), and non-linear complexity on 6 channels. This method reached a False Reject error (FRE) ranging from 0 to 1.5%. the EEG signal recorded during the performance of three mental tasks to identify six subjects. Power spectral density feature using Welch algorithm is extracted from the EEG beta waves this was proposed by (Hema el al., 2008). Feed Forward Neural Classifier is used to achieve an average authentication rate of 97%.

The use of PSD as the feature, the statistical framework is done based on Gaussian Mixture Models (GMM) and Maximum a Posteriori Model (MAPM) Adaptation on speaker and face authentication. The potential of their method is shown by simulations using strict train and test protocols and results. Person identification based on spectral information is extracted from the EEG is addressed by (Poulos et al., 2001). The proposed method has yielded correct classification scores in the range of 80% to 97% showing evidence that the EEG carries genetic information for person identification. Research proposed (Ravi et al., 2005) utilized the 40 Hz EEG oscillations related to the visual processing for subject identification. Visual Evoked Potential (VEP) was recorded from 20 subjects while they were looking at a picture. PCA was applied; fuzzy ARTMAP, k-nearest neighbor, and back propagation network classifiers were used attaining performance of up to 95% with 61 electrodes were used to record the EEG signals.

The 40 Hz EEG oscillations related to the visual processing for subject identification. VEP was recorded from 20 subjects while they were looking at a picture. PCA was applied; Fuzzy Adaptive Resonance Theory (F-ARTMAP), k-nearest neighbor, and back propagation network classifiers were used for identification and attaining performance of 95% with 61 electrodes EEG recordings (Ravi et al., 2005). Biometric identification systems are summarized by (Poulus et al., 1999a; Poulus et al., 1999b). Recorded EEG signals from 1 channel of 4 subjects resting with eyes closed. They applied parametric processing and computational Geometry and achieved 84% and 91% respectively. EEG as an authentication tool which is used by (Riera et al., 2008). Data collected from 51 subjects and 36 intruders. Equal error rate (EER) of 3.4% is obtained, True Acceptance Rate (TAR) of 96.6% and a False Acceptance Rate (FAR) of 3.4%. (Poulos et al., 1998; Poulos et al., 1999) proposed a method to distinguish an individual from the rest using EEG signals. They performed a parametric spectral analysis of α band EEG signals by fitting to them a linear all-pole autoregressive model. The coefficients of the fitted model were then used as features for the identification component. In (Poulos et al., 1998) the identification component was built with computational geometric algorithms and (Poulos et al., 1999) they changed it to a neural network, namely for a Kohonen's Linear Vector Quantizer (Kohonenet al., 1989). The cerebral activity was recorded from subjects at rest, with closed eyes using single channel EEG for three minutes.

Maximum a Posterior (MAP) trained Gaussian models on the EEG classification. Band data were preprocessed by a spline Laplacian filter prior to the PSD computation. Authentication possibilities were tested; identification scores in the ranges of 60% to 100% were achieved. Interestingly, the authors observed a degradation of the identification performance over days (Marcel et al., 2007). Biometric identification with EEG were recorded over 14 electrodes placed over the whole scalp; EEG is parameterized using a 1358 dimensional feature vector composed of autoregressive coefficients, Power Spectral Density, integrated spectral power, inter hemispheric power differences, and inter hemispheric linear complexity. SVM is used for EEG data classification. Classification scores in the range of 97% is achieved (Ashby et al., 2011). A multimodal authentication algorithm based on EEG and Electrocardiogram (ECG) signal is done by (Riera et al., 2010). They conducted tests on 40 healthy subjects. Each subject was required to sit in a comfortable armchair, to relax, be quiet and open their eyes. Features were extracted using auto regression and Fourier Transform. The classifier used in the authentication process is the classical fisher's discriminate analysis. True Acceptance Rate (TAR) of 71.9% and a False Acceptance Rate (FAR) of 21.8%.

EEG as a potential biometric for personal Identification has been studied by Marios S.Poulos since 1998, and colleagues were EEG biometrics when in 1999. They presented an automatic person identification system that was based on EEG signals acquired from four subjects in a resting state with closed eyes, closed eye position and the resting state of the brain wave acquisition protocol has used for biometric authentication. Autoregressive (AR) stochastic modeling and polynomial regression based classification with an accuracy of 97% (Daria La Rocca et al., 2012). A short time Principal Component Analysis on overlapping window segments and non overlapping window segment is performed to extract the feature. A Recurrent Neural Network (RNN) based classification of EEG features is proposed by (Hema et al., 2007). The results validate the feasibility of classifying EEG patterns related to mental task. Average classification accuracy of 97.5% was obtainable.

A multiple mental thought authentication model. The experiment was conducted on four subjects. An Electro-Cap elastic electrode cap was used to record EEG signals from positions C3, C4, P3, P4, O1 and O2 defined by the 10-20 system of electrode placement. Six, AR coefficients were obtained for each channel, giving a total of 36 feature vector for each EEG segment for a mental thought. Linear Discriminate Classifier was used to classify the EEG feature vectors; LDC is a linear classification method that is computationally attractive as compared to other classifiers like artificial neural network (Palaniappan et al., 2006). LVQ for user identification. The algorithm was conducted on a dataset of 8 subjects. Linear magnitude spectra of the single segments were computed by Fast Fourier Transform Hamming window was used. The LVQ neural network is a self–organizing neural network, with an added second layer for vector classification intended to be used by unlabeled training data. Hence LVQ network is a kind of nearest-neighbor classifier; it does not make clusters, but the algorithm search through the weights of connections between input layer neurons and output map neurons. The best classification rate was around 80% (Cempirek et al., 2007).

The Common Spatial Patterns (CSP) are employed to carry out energy feature extraction by (Sun et al., 2008). The system was tested on 9 subjects. The task was to imagine moving his or her left or right index finger in response to a highly predictable visual cue. Based on these features, neural network classifiers can be learned. Neural networks of one hidden layer and one output layer for experiments. The results showed that imagining left index finger movements is more appropriate for personal identification. The left index movement gave a classification accuracy of 95.6%. A Multimodal authentication algorithm based on EEG and Electrocardiogram (ECG) signals proposed by (Riera et al., 2008). They conducted the test on 40 healthy subjects. Three features were selected from the synchronicity features, namely; Mutual information, Coherence and Correlation measures. The classifier used in the authentication process is the classical Fisher's Discriminant Analysis, Four different discriminant functions were used (Linear, Diagonal Linear, quadratic, diagonal quadratic). After combining the 2 signals (EEG and ECG) the TAR is 97.9% and the FAR is 0.82%.

Wavelet Packet Transform (WPT) was used for feature extraction of the relevant frequency bands from the raw EEG signals. The two classifiers used were Radial Basis Function Neural Network (RBFNN) and Multilayer Perceptron Back propagation Neural Network. RBF Neural Network has better performance as compared to MLP-BP NN with Resilient back propagation method for classification. Average accuracy was obtained 100% by using RBFNN classifier (Vijay Khare et al., 2010). EEG signals were measured using 64 electrodes and sampled at 256 Hz for 1 second. Univariate autoregressive model is used as feature extractor and model order of 4 appeared to be optimal. Subject verification is done using a linear SVM classifier. The subjects were identifiable to 99.76% accuracy (Katharine Brigham et al., 2010).

The data collected from two subjects were used in this study. Subjects were aged between 21 and 48 years. EEG signals are obtained from two subjects. On performing the PCA transform 6 features per window matrix per task. The RNN is trained using the Practical Swam Optimization (PSO) algorithm to classify the EEG signals into two mental tasks. Average classification accuracies obtained with the PSO RNN vary from 82.5% to 93% (Hema et al., 2008). The eye blinking signal is extracted and applied for identification and verification tasks. The raw signal was collected from 25 healthy, non-alcoholics, subjects. Four groups of features (G1, G2, G3, and G4) were extracted based on time delineation of the eye blinking waveform. Different classifiers like Vector Quantization (VQ), Gaussian Mixture Modeling (GMM), and Discriminant Analysis (DA) based on linear or quadratic boundaries, and SVM were tested for the proposed system by (Chen et al., 2006). Identified subjects with best accuracy of 95.3%.

Data were collected from 10 male subjects while resting with eyes open and eyes closed in 5 separate sessions conducted over a course of two weeks. Features were extracted using the wavelet packet decomposition subsequently; the neural network algorithm is used to classify the feature vectors. Results show that 2– channel system using only the C3 and C4 channels outperformed then 4– channel biometrics system with a classification accuracy of 81% (Muhammad Kamil Abdullah et al., 2010).

Gamma Band Spectral Power (GBSP) features extracted from VEP signals recorded from 61 channels while subjects perceived a picture. Researchers applied PCA to reduce noise and background EEG effects as the first step. During the second step, the GBSP of each channel was normalized by the total GBSP. For the classification, namely Simplified Fuzzy ARTMAP (SFA), Linear Discriminant (LD) and k-Nearest Neighbor (KNN). KNN gave improved results through the use of PCA with classification performance of 96.5% (Palaniappan et al., 2005). The effectiveness of the EEG as a biometric for the person identification of individual subject in a pool of 40 normal subject mention by (Paranjape et at. 2001). The AR coefficients in these models are then evaluated of their biometric potential. Discriminant function applied to the model coefficients are used to examine to which the subjects in the data pool can be identified. In this data pool 90% correctly identified. Brain

Computer Interface (BCI) research from laboratory to real word application study conducted by (Wenjie XU et al., 2004) presents a high accuracy of the EEG signal classification method. EEG signal into a spatial pattern applies the Radial Basis Function (RBF) feature selection method to generate robust feature. Classification is performed by the SVM which obtained a classification rate of 90%.

Researches (Poulos et al., 1999) experimented classification of a person as one of a finite set of known persons. In the tests they recorded 45 EEG features from each of 4 individuals (the X set) and one EEG feature from each of 75 individuals (the non-X set). The neural network was trained using 20 features from each X member and 30 features from non-X members. Then the system was used to classify the remaining 25 features of each X member and the 45 features from the remaining non-X members. This process was repeated for all the 4 X members, attaining a correct persons verification score between 72% and 84%. EEG-base person authentication is first proposed by (Marcel et al., 2007). They proposed the use of PSD as the feature, and a statistical framework based on GMM and MAP Model Adaptation.

2.11 MULTIMODAL BIOMETRICS BASED ON IDENTIFICATION AND VERIFICATION SYSTEM

The framework for multimodal biometric person authentication developed by (Jain et. al., 2004). Even though some of the traits offering good performance in terms of reliability and accuracy, none of the biometrics is 100% accurate. With the increasing global need for security, the demand for robust automatic person recognition systems is evident. For applications involving the flow of confidential information, the authentication accuracy of the system is always the priority concern. From this basic reason the use of multimodal biometrics is encouraged. Multi biometrics are an integrated prototype system embedding different types of biometrics. Multimodal biometric fusion and identity authentication technique help to achieve an increase in performance of identity authentication system. A Bimodal biometric systems using speech and face features and tested its performance under degraded condition. Speaker Verification (SV) system is built using Mel-Frequency Cepstral Coefficients (MFCC) followed by delta and delta-delta for feature extraction and Gaussian Mixture Model (GMM) for modeling. A Face Verification (FV) system is built using the combination of Principal Component Analysis (PCA) and Linear Discriminant Analysis (LDA). Sum rule is used for the fusion of the biometric scores. The performance of the SV system under the degraded condition is also checked. All the experimental results are shown upon a subset of IITG-DIT M4 multi-biometric database. The complementary information derived from the speech biometric at training stage is used to further decrease the FV error rate, which is termed as Cohort fed FV system. Finally, we propose an improved bimodal person authentication system using SV and Cohort fed FV biometric systems (Soyuj Kumar Sahoo et al., 2005).

Electrocardiogram (ECG) and Phonocardiogram (PCG) signals are not only useful for medical purposes, but can also be applied for biometric identification and verification. A group of 20 subjects are modeled by the system, and for heart sound. The database is divided into groups of training and test data. Speech: The same set of clients and impostors are used in speaker recognition. Mel Frequency Cestrum Coefficients (MFCC) were used as the feature representation of the heart and speech signals. 12 MFCCs per frame are used for the classification step. Speaker Identification (SI) model is 99.3% and Electrocardiogram Identification (ECGI) 98.5%. From the result speaker Identification out performed ECGI (Osamah Al-Hamdani et al., 2013).

From the survey, it is observed that the limitations using the conventional biometrics include that they are unique identifiers, but they are not confidential and neither secret to an individual. For example, people leave their physical prints of finger on everything they touch, iris patterns can be observed anywhere they look, faces are visible, and voices are being recorded. The presence of biometric prints publicly, offering intruders to lift these prints and copy them as real, thus spoofs the system. One of the main advantages of using EEG signals as biometric is that the reproduction of the EEG signals is very difficult until the same individual is not called for the re-enrollment. Therefore, the proposed methods using the EEG as biometric are sufficiently non vulnerable to spoof attacks.

2.12 SUMMARY

This chapter provides an overview of EEG signal classification and also provides necessary background knowledge related to the EEG. Then this chapter discusses about the classification of EEG signals and also reviews which methods were used for the EEG signal classification in the previous study. From the literature review of the EEG signal classification, it can be concluded that there are still some limitations associated with the existing methods. Hence developing feature extraction and classification algorithms are needed for person authentication. The experimental setup and data acquisition for single channel and two channel system procedure are discussed in the following chapter.

CHAPTER 3

DATA COLLECTION AND PREPROCESSING

3.1 INTRODUCTION

This chapter presents the recording of EEG signals, brain signature, bio amplifier, electrode placement and measurement, experimental setup and protocols. EEG signal acquisition for single channel and two channel system and also pre-processing techniques are briefly discussed below.

3.2 RECORDING OF EEG SIGNAL

EEG recording is technically difficult, mainly because of the small size of the voltage signals which are typically 50 µV peak-to-peak. These signals are small because the recording electrodes are separated from the brain surface of the scalp, and a layer of cerebral spinal fluid. A specially designed amplifier, such as the Bio Amp built into the Power Lab, is essential to record EEGs. It is also important to use electrodes made of the right material and the connection should be in a proper way. Even with these precautions, recordings may be spoiled by a range of unwanted interfering influences, known as artifacts. In this laboratory ,we record EEG activity with two electrodes: a frontal electrode on the forehead, and an occipital electrode on the scalp at the back of the head. A third (ground or earth) electrode is also attached to reduce electrical interference. In clinical EEG, it is usual to record many channels of activity from multiple recording electrodes which is placed over the head.

3.3 ORIGIN OF THE EEG BRAIN SIGNATURE

Our brain is connected to the outside world thought the sensory organs which acts as transducers converting physical energy such as auditory pressure wanes or light waves into a series of which are conveyed along the nerve fibers to the brain. The amplitude of the sensory stimulus is encoded or represented a plus repetition frequency. The brain not only responds to sensory stimulus, but also thinks. Both activities invoke cognitive processing at the neural level, thus both are reflected in EEG. The neurons or nerve cell is the basic building block of the nervous system. An aggregation of these neurons is arranged in many complicated ways to process information and to take decisions. The nerve cell is a membrane that separates two media the cytoplasm and the extracellular fluid. The ionic concentrations are considerably different between these media. The membrane is normally polarized at a potential difference of approximately 10-100 mV with the inside negative relative to the outside. Dendrites carry information to the neuron. An axon carries information away from the neurons. These potential are depolarizing, their collective action increases or decreases respectively the probability of the cell discharging a pike along its axon to the next cell. The axon is a inter collecting cable between the cells, but these cables are not passive instead the plus is regenerated along the axon analogous to repeaters in telephone lines. Along the axon synaptic junctions at either outer cell bodies or in the dendrites or in other neurons. These synaptic junctions which may be as many as 1000 per axon conduct in only one direction. When the nerve impulse arrives at one of these junctions its triggers the releases of a chemical transmitter that fires the effect of the nerve pulse across the junction by chemical. The chemical in turn produces graded slow potential, called post synaptic potential, which may be as large as 30 mV in the recipient cell and its dendrites.

3.4 BRAIN SIGNATURE ACQUISITION PROTOCOL

3.4.1 10-20 Electrode Placement and Measurement

In order to perform a consistent testing for the EEG signal recording system is developed which would describe the locations on electrodes in human skull known as 10-20 system of electrode placement shown in Figure 3.1 International 10-20 electrode placement system is found on the relationship of a skull and the corresponding cortical anatomy. Electrodes are placed on the scalp which records the information using a machine called an electroencephalographic. There are three types of electrode connections found namely

❖ **Bipolar:** Calculating the difference between the nearest electrodes.

❖ **Referential:** Calculating the difference with reference to the ear lobe so a node at the right side of the head uses reference of the right ear, and left with the left ear.

❖ **Common Reference:** Calculating the difference between the single electrode references for all electrodes. Based on the mental tasks that the user will perform the activities that should be expected at certain channels which reflect the part of the brain responsible for this activity.

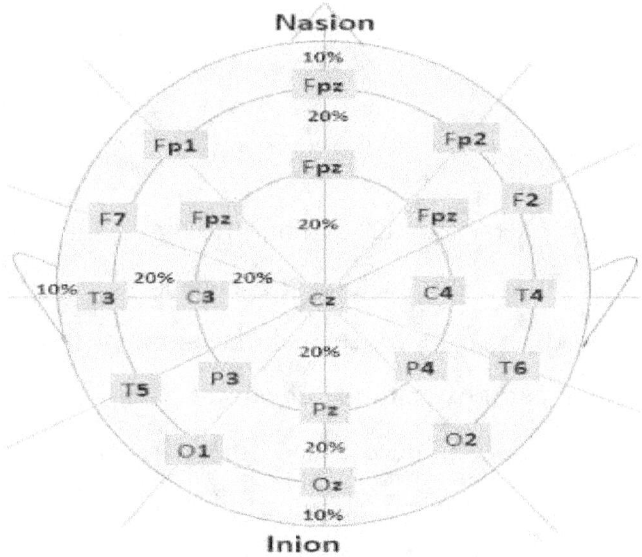

Figure 3.1 10-20 System of Electrode Placement

Important features are needed to be considered in the development of the 10-20 system which is in the standard format of 10-20 system based on the relationship between the location of an electrode and the underlying area of cerebral cortex.

♦ Each point indicates the possible electrode position.

♦ Each electrode sites have a letter to identify the lobes and a number or another letter to identify the hemisphere location.

♦ The letters F, T, C, P and O refer to Frontal, Temporal, Central, Parietal and Occipital lobes of the brain respectively.

♦ Even numbers 2, 4, 6 and 8 are used to represent electrode positions on the right hemisphere, whereas odd numbers 1, 3, 5 and 7 are used to represent the positioning on the left hemisphere.

◆ The Z refers to an electrode placement on the middle line.

The exact measurement of electrode placement is done by using a tape measurement from midpoint of both eyebrows till back the head where could feel a bump. Most individual measurements are in the range of 36 cm. From here, divide the value into 2 and it is the CZ point. To get the FZ and PZ point is 20% of the total range from CZ. The others are obtained as 10% of the total range.

3.4.2 Surface Electrodes

Surface EEG electrodes provide a non-invasive technique for measurement and detection of EEG signal. The theory behind these electrodes is that they form a chemical equilibrium between the detecting surface and the skin of the body through electrolytic conduction, so that current can flow into the electrode. These electrodes are simple and very easy to implement. Application of needle and fine wire electrodes require strict medical supervision and certification. Surface EEG electrodes require no such formalities. Surface EEG has some limitations as well. Since these electrodes are applied on the skin, they are generally used for scalp skin and muscles only (Nuria Masso et al., 2010).

Figure 3.2 Ag-Agcl Disc Electrodes.

Commonly used scalp electrode consists of Silver chloride (Ag-Agcl) disks less than 3 mm in diameter, with long, flexible leads that can be plugged into an amplifier. Silver chloride

(Agcl) Figure 3.2 is performed in the common neurophysiologies application. Because Ag is a slightly soluble salt, Agcl quickly saturates and comes to equilibrium. Therefore Agcl is a good metal for metallic skin-surface electrode.

3.4.3 Experimental Setup and Electrode Attachment

Make sure the Power Lab is turned off and the USB cable is connected to the computer. Connect the 5 Lead Shielded Bio Amp Cable to the Bio Amp Connector on the front and back panel of the Power Lab. The hardware needs to be connected before you open the settings file. Attach the leads of the EEG flat electrodes to the earth, CH1 (channel 1) NEG (negative) and POS (positive) pins closest to the labeled side on the Bio Amp Cable. If channel 1 is "positive" it leads to the frontal location and if channel 1 is "negative" it leads to the occipital location. The Earth will lead to the nasion. Remove all the ornaments from the volunteer's face, ears, and neck. Use a ballpoint pen to mark a small cross on the skin at the skull. Abrade the skin with Abrasive Gel or Pad. This is important as abrasion helps to reduce the skin's resistance. Check that all three electrodes are properly connected to the volunteer and the Bio Amp Cable before proceeding. Turn on the Power Lab.

3.5 BRAIN SIGNATURE ACQUISITION

All subjects were first time EEG users, whose age ranging from 18-45 years, they are from university and college. During signal acquisition it was ensured that the subject did not smoke few hours prior to data collection and all subjects were healthy and free from any medication. Subjects were informed about the purpose and procedure before the experiment. In order to reduce electrode-scalp interface impedance, subject scalp cleaned with skin preparation gel. Then the electrode is placed on the scalp using EEG paste. Electrodes are placed as per the international $10 - 20$ system. The subjects are seated comfortably in a sound controlled booth with dim lighting in front of a computer screen, which conducted the subjects throughout the experiment. No overt movements were made during the performance and good motivation was given during the experiments. The subjects were also asked to refrain from blinking as much as possible during the experiment. The subjects were asked to spell their names and they performed it correctly. Similarly, many other activities like relax, read, maths etc were done with the subject. Each trial was taken with 5 minutes break.

3.5.1 BRAIN SIGNAL ACQUISITION PROTOCOL

The protocol for the four biometric tasks performed by the individuals using single channel and two channel systems are detailed below.

Task1- Relax: The subject is requested to sit in a relaxed manner. The subject should be still without moving the entire body for 10 sec. This task is used as a baseline measure of the EEG.

Task2- Read: The subject is shown a typed card with tongue twister sentences and they are requested to read the sentence mentally without vocalizing. The sample of reading is attached in Appendix A.

Task3- Maths Activity: The subject is given five non trivial multiplication problems, and is asked to solve them for 10 sec without moving the entire body. The sample of multiplication is attached in Appendix B.

Task 4- Spell: The subject is shown a typed card with his/her name and is requested to spell his/her name mentally without vocalization and overt movements. The sample of names attached in Appendix C.

3.5.2 BRAIN SIGNATURE ACQUISITION FOR SINGLE CHANNEL SYSTEM

The EEG signal is acquired using three non invasive electrodes. The electrodes are gold plated cup shaped discs placed at F4, O2 and FP1 location based on the international 10-20 electrode placement system. Each electrode site has a letter to identify the lobe, along with a number or another letter to identify the hemispheric location. FP1 is the earth electrode which is placed at the center of the forehead. This electrode is used as reference. F4 and O2 electrodes are placed on right side of the forehead. The left and right side electrode is connected to the channel1 based on the positive and negative terminal. The entire subject's head measured were 36 cm. This value is divided by 2. From here 20% of 36 cm is calculated to locate FZ and PZ point. Then, 10% of 36 cm is taken to locate F4. Again 3.6 cm measured facing downward to locate O2. Figure 3.3 shown the position used for data collection. Since, the voltage acquired is in microvolt, a gel is applied to the cup sized gold plated electrodes disk to utilize absorption voltages from the scalp. The subjects were seated comfortably in a noise free room. The subject did not make any overt movement and performed tasks mentally. The subjects were requested to perform four biometric tasks. Each task was repeated for ten trials and each trial was recorded for 10 sec. The sampling frequency ratio is 200 Hz. The data were collected in two sessions on different days. 40 data samples were collected per subjects and a total of 2000 data samples are acquired from all 50 subjects.

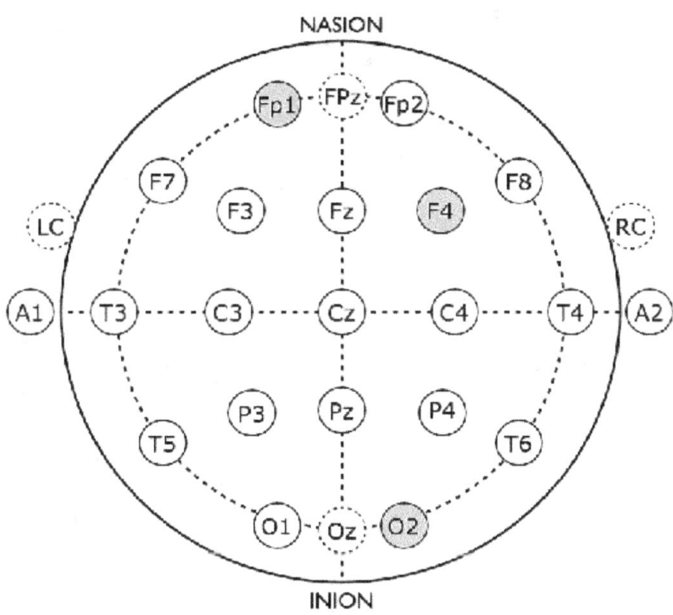

Figure 3.3 Electrode Location for Single Channel System

3.5.4 BRAIN SIGNATURE ACQUISITION FOR TWO CHANNEL SYSTEMS

The EEG signal is acquired using five non invasive electrodes. The electrodes are gold plated cup shaped discs placed at O1, O2, F3, F4 and FP1 location based on the international 10-20 electrode placement system. FP1 is the earth electrode which is placed at center of the forehead. This electrode is used as reference. O1, O2, F3 and F4 electrodes are placed at the left and right of the forehead. The left and right electrode is connected to the channel1 and channel2 based on the positive and negative terminal. The entire subject head measured was 36 cm. This value is divided by 2. From here 20% of 36 cm is calculated to locate FZ and PZ point. Then 10% of 36 cm taken to locate F3 and F4. Again 3.6 cm measured facing downward to locate O1 and O2. Figure 3.4 shown the position used for data collection. Since, the voltage acquired is in microvolt, a gel is applied to the cup sized gold plated electrodes disk to utilize absorption voltages from the scalp. The subject were requested to perform four mental tasks and data acquired from the average of five electrodes O1, O2, F3, F4 and FP1 recorded for 10 sec and each task was repeated ten times per sessions. 40 data sets were collected from each subject for four tasks. The sampling frequency ratio is 200 Hz. 200*10= 2000 data samples were collected. Data was collected at two sessions on different days. The data acquisitions for 25 subjects are shown in Figure 3.4.

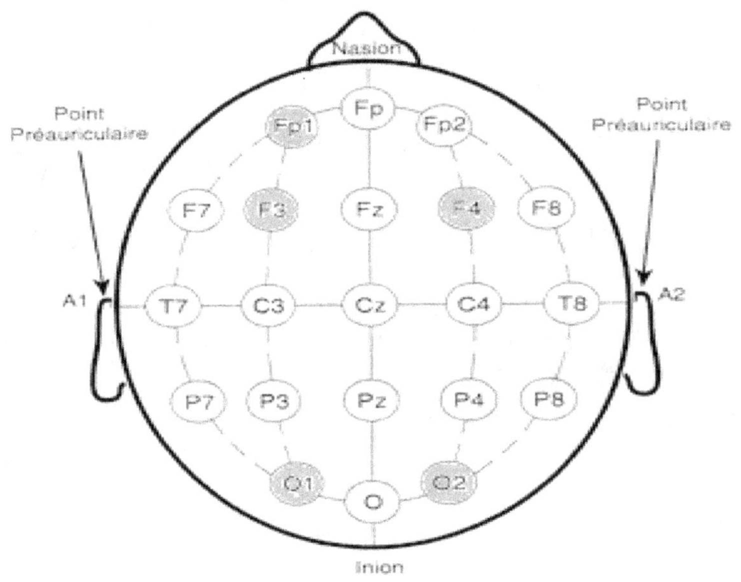

Figure 3.4 Electrode Location for Two Channel System

3.6 RAW EEG SIGNALS FOR THE FOUR TASKS

The raw EEG signals for four biometric tasks using single and two channel systems are shown in Figure 3.5. Namely maths, read, relax and spell tasks are performed. The EEG is collected from individuals having 2000 samples of a healthy subject and the length of the recorded signals was 10 sec. X and Y axis represents time (sec) and amplitude (mV) respectively. The simulation part is carried out in Matlab platform.

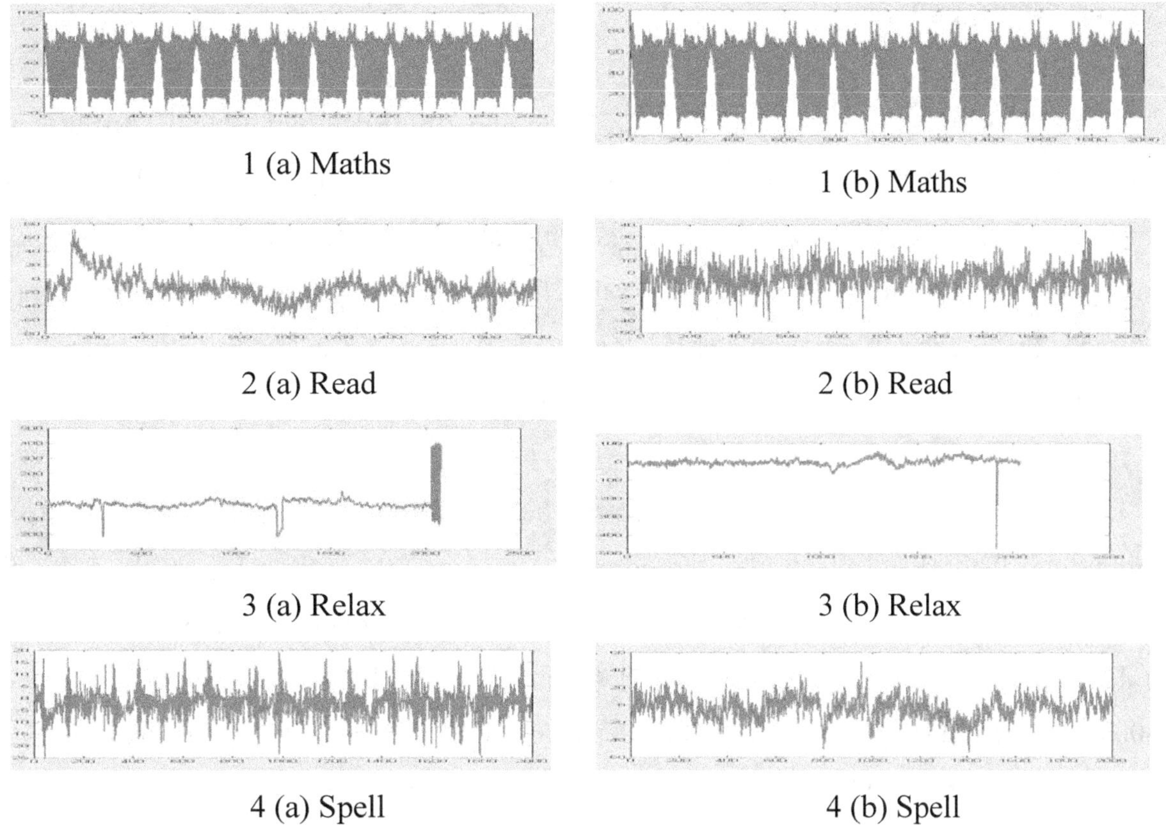

1 (a) Maths   1 (b) Maths

2 (a) Read   2 (b) Read

3 (a) Relax   3 (b) Relax

4 (a) Spell   4 (b) Spell

Figure 3.5 EEG Signals for (A) Channel1 and (B) Channel2 System Using Bioamplifier

3.7 PREPROCESSING

EEG signal preprocessing means that the raw EEG signal analysis are processed to remove the noise signal. Signal pre-processing is necessary to maximize the SNR because there are many noise sources encountered with the EEG signal. Once the data have been acquired, they are generally preprocessed in order to remove the noise signals. Noise sources can be non-neural (eye movements, muscular activity, 50 Hz power-line noise) or neural (EEG features other than those used for control). Mostly as the noise signals are greater in amplitude and before analysis, it is necessary to improve the quality of the signal by preprocessing the raw data.

3.8 ARTIFACTS IN EEG

EEG signals are very weak (ranging from 1 to 100 mV); they can easily be affected by other sources. An EEG signal that does not originate from the brain is called an artifact. Artifacts can be divided into two categories: Physiologic and Non-Physiologic. Physiological: (a) Eye artifacts (including eyeball, ocular muscles and eyelid) (b) Electrocardiography (ECG) artifacts (c) Electromyography (EMG) artifacts (d) Gloss kinetic artifacts (minor tongue movements) (Delorme et al., 2007; Sadasivan et al., 1995).

Non-Physiological: (a) Movement by the patient (b) Power line (50/60 Hz) (c) Poor grounding of the EEG electrodes. To correct, or remove the artifacts from the EEG signal, many techniques have been developed in both, time and frequency domains. More recently Independent Component Analysis (ICA) (Akhtar et al., 2012) WT (Senthil Kumar et al., 2009) WT combined with ICA (Ghandeharion et al., 2009) and Autoregressive Moving Average Exogenous (ARMAX) (Hass et al., 2003; Park et al., 2002) have been applied too, to remove artifacts from EEG.

3.9 COMMON ARTIFACTS IN EEG RECORDS

The most common artifacts in the EEG signal appear during the acquisition due to different causes, like bad electrodes location, power line, electrode impedance, cable movements, low battery, etc. EEG signals are often contaminated with 50 or 60 Hz line frequency intervention from electric wires, light fluorescents and other equipments which are captured by the electrodes and acquisition system. The ignition of light of fluorescents usually causes artificial spikes in the EEG. They are distributed in several channels of EEG and can make a mistake in the analysis of the record (Sanei et al., 2007). Physiological artifacts, that is, bioelectrical signals from other parts of the body (heart and muscle activity, eye blink and eyeball movement) which are registered in the EEG (Sornmo et al., 2005). The muscle disturbances are introduced in the EEG by involuntary muscle contractions of the patient, thus generating an Electromyography (EMG) signal present in the EEG recording. The problem of those artifacts is that they can make a mistake in the analysis of an EEG record, either in automatic method or in visual inspection by specialist (Wang et. al., 2008).

3.10 CHEBYSHEV FILTER

Temporal filtering using a Chebyshev type 2 band filter is applied to extract the three rhythms from raw and segmented EEG. The transfer function of a type 2 Chebyshev filter as given by

$$H_a(s) = \frac{P_a(s)}{d_a(s)} = k\frac{s - z1s - z2 \dots s - zN}{s - p1s - p2 \dots s - pN} \tag{3.1}$$

Where K is the gain factor, N is the data length, vector Z and P, provide the locations of Zero and poles respectively. The pass band and the stop band of a Chebyshev filter produce smaller absolute errors and faster execution speeds than a Butterworth filter. Minimizing peak error in the stop band instead of the pass band is advantages of Chebyshev filter 2 filters over Chebyshev filter. Chebyshev type 2 filter have an equi-ripple magnitude response in the stop band instead of the pass band. Chebyshev type 2 filter have a monotonically decreasing magnitude response in the pass band instead of the stop band. Chebyshev type 2 filter have the following characteristics:

a) Minimization of peak error in the stop band
b) Equi-ripple magnitude response in the stop band
c) Monotonically decreasing magnitude response in the pass band
d) Sharper roll than butter worth filters. Chebyshev type 2 filter ha the same advantages over butter worth filter that Chebyshev filter have a sharper transition between the pass band and the stop band with a lower order filter, resulting in a smaller absolute error and faster execution speed.

3.11 EEG PREPROCESSING

Once the data has been acquired, they are generally preprocessed in order to clean the signal and to enhance relevance information embedded in the signal. A notch filter is applied to remove the 50 Hz power line artifacts from the EEG signal. The raw EEG signals are acquired and segmented into four frequency bands, namely delta (0.5-3 Hz), theta (3-7 Hz), alpha (7-12 Hz) and beta (12-40 Hz). Among the four, alpha and beta are seen in the conscious state of a human. Hence, we consider the frequency bands alpha and beta from the original frequency bands. The EEG signal is band pass filtered using twelve frequency bands from the alpha and beta rhythms of 7 Hz to 42 Hz with a bandwidth of 3 Hz. Chebyshev band pass filter to apply the segment the signal. The 12 band pass signals are (7-10) Hz, (10-13) Hz, (13-16) Hz, (16-19) Hz, (19-21) Hz, (21-24) Hz, (24-27) Hz, (27-30) Hz, (30-33) Hz, (33-36) Hz, (36-39) Hz and (39-42) Hz. This segmentation is used to remove the lower range noise frequencies from 0.1 to 6 Hz arising due to EOG signals and EMG signals above 43 Hz. 12 signal segments are obtained from the pre-processed EEG signals.

3.12 SUMMARY

This chapter describes briefly about the data collection technique and the preprocessing methods followed during the data acquisition process. The standard 10-20 electrode placement measurement is followed for the recording of the EEG brain signals. Four biometric tasks, namely read, relax, maths and spell are performed by the individuals. The EEG acquisition is done for both single and two channel system. 50 subjects took part in a single channel system experiment, whereas 25 subjects took part in a two channel system experiment. In a single channel system only three electrodes are used and in double channel system five electrodes are used for data acquisition. The raw EEG signal for the four tasks, namely read, relax, maths and spell activity are shown in Figure 3.5. The preprocessing techniques for EEG data are discussed.

CHAPTER 4

FEATURE EXTRACTION AND CLASSIFICATION

4.1. INTRODUCTION

This chapter briefly describes about the techniques of feature extraction in which power spectral density is used. The three methods of PSD are a parametric, non parametric and high resolution method. The neural network models are used for the classification purpose. Here two neural network models, namely Feed Forward Neural Network (FFNN) and Recurrent Neural Network (RNN) are used. These methods are discussed briefly.

4.2 FEATURE EXTRACTION

The input data to an algorithm is too big to be processed and if it is suspected to be notoriously redundant then the input data will be transformed into a reduced representation set of features. Transforming the input data into the set of features is called feature extraction. If the features extracted are carefully chosen it is expected that the features set will extract the relevant information from the input data in order to perform the desired task using this reduced representation instead of the full size input. Many different features have been thought to be extracted from EEG signals. PSD of the segmented signals is estimated and used as features. PSD describes how the energy of a signal or a time series is distributed with frequency. The six PSD algorithms, namely Covariance, Modified Covariance, MUSIC, Burg, Welch and Yule-Walker are used.

4.3 POWER SPECTRUM DENSITY (PSD)

One of the most important applications in Digital Signal Processing (DSP) is the power spectrum of signals which are periodic or random. A spectrum is presentation of magnitude against frequency of one parameter. The PSD explains how the power or energy of a signal is distributed across frequency. Power spectrum is commonly defined as the Fourier

Transform of the autocorrelation function. In continuous and discrete notation, the power equation becomes:

$$PS(f) = \int_{O}^{T} r_{xx}(\tau) e^{-2\pi f T \tau} d\tau \qquad (4.1)$$

$$PS(f) = \int_{n=0}^{N-1} r_{xx}(\tau) e^{-j2\pi fTs} \qquad (4.2)$$

Where $r_{xx}(n)$ is autocorrelation function. Since auto correlation functions has odd symmetry, the sine terms and Eq. 4.2 can be simplified to include only real cosine terms.

$$PS(f) = \int_{0}^{T} r_{xx}(\tau) \cos(2\pi mfrTt)\, dr \qquad (4.3)$$

$$PS(f) = \int_{n=0}^{N-1} r_{xx}(\tau) \cos(2\pi mfrTs) \qquad (4.4)$$

These equations are continuous and discrete form is sometimes referred to as the cosine transforms. This approach to evaluating the power spectrum has lost favor to the so-called direct approach, given by equation 4.5 below primilarly because of the efficiency of Fast Fourier Transform (Kay et al., 1988).

The direct approach is motivated by the fact that the energy contained as an analog signal, xt is related to magnitude of the signal squared, integrated over time

$$E = \int_{-\infty}^{\infty} |xt|^2\, dt \qquad (4.5)$$

By an extension of Parseval theorem it is easy to show that

$$\int_{-\infty}^{\infty} |xt|^2\, dt = \int_{-\infty}^{\infty} |Xf|^2\, df \qquad (4.6)$$

Hence, equals the energy density function over frequency also referred to as the energy spectral density, the PSD or simply power spectrum. In the direct approach, the power spectrum is calculated as the magnitude square of the Fourier Transform of the waveform of interest:

$$PS(f) = |Xf^2| \qquad\qquad (4.7)$$

The PSD is computed as the distribution of power per unit frequency. Power spectral density is normally used for signal feature extraction. Hence PSD is frequency domain analysis.

The performance of various PSD estimation techniques are parametric method, non-parametric methods and high resolution method are compared to different epoch lengths in case of real signal (Akankshya Shradhanjali et al., 2013).

1. Parametric methods are based on the estimation of a linear time invariant system from noise by autoregressive-moving-average (ARMA) model such as Covariance, Burg, Modified Covariance and Yule–Walker. These methods have improved performances, although they are affected by the SNR level.

2. Nonparametric methods include conventional Fourier analysis, optimal band pass filtering analysis, Periodogram, and Welch. These methods do not solve the limits of the frequency resolution of the classical Fourier analysis.

3. High-resolution methods include techniques such as MUSIC and Eigenvector. These methods can detect frequencies with low SNR and compute the autocorrelation matrix, and its Eigen-values can be separated into signal and noise spaces. These methods define a Pseudo-spectrum function with large peaks that are subspace frequency estimates, and they are commonly used in the communication area. They have been recently introduced into the area of induction machine diagnosis by the application of the MUSIC method.

4.3.1 Parametric Spectral Analysis Method

Autoregressive (AR) method is a commonly used method. The most important advantage of AR model parameter provides stable statistical estimates with high frequency resolution. For this reason, in the analysis we have used Burg, Covariance, Modified Covariance and Yule-Walker methods. Estimation accuracy of parameters in AR signal models is a suggested matter and estimations are found by solving linear equation. The magnitude of the signal in the period given in the AR method is acquired by the total no of the magnitudes of previous samples and in addition, it minimizes the errors. Model sequence is connected to AR factors. Selection of the degree of AR model is very important and is defined by different criteria. Though a number of methods are used to determine the degree of the model.

$$AIC(p) = ln\sigma^2 + \frac{2p}{N} \tag{4.8}$$

Here σ^2 is the estimated variance of linear estimating error and N is the length of the data. With the increase in the AR model parameter, σ^2 diminishes and therefore, $ln\sigma^2$ diminishes as well. In this case, p must be valid as minimum (Djuric et, al. 1999; Keith et al., 1993; Dhaparidze et al., 1983).

4.3.1.1 Covariance Method

The Covariance method for AR spectral estimation is based on minimizing the forward prediction error. This method fits an autoregressive model to the signal by minimizing the forward prediction error in the least squares sense. In the covariance method all the data points are needed to compute the prediction error power estimate. No zeroing of the data is necessary. The AR parameter estimates the solution of the equations and can be written (Lawrence et al., 1987; Kay et al., 1988).

$$\begin{bmatrix} c(1,0) \\ \dots\dots \\ c(p,0) \end{bmatrix} + \begin{bmatrix} c(1,1) \dots\dots c(1,p) \\ \dots\dots\dots \\ c(p,1) \dots c(p,p) \end{bmatrix} \begin{bmatrix} \hat{a}(1) \\ \dots\dots \\ \hat{a}(p) \end{bmatrix} = \begin{bmatrix} 0 \\ \dots \\ 0 \end{bmatrix} \tag{4.11}$$

Where

$$c(j,k) = \frac{1}{N-P}\sum_{n=P}^{N-1} x^*\,(n-jx(n\text{-}k) \tag{4.12}$$

From Eq. (4.11) the AR parameter estimates are found as:

$$a = -c_p^{-1}c_p \tag{4.13}$$

This statement is acquired and white noise variance is

$$\sigma^2 = c[0,0] + \sum_{k=1}^{p} a[k]c(0,k) \tag{4.14}$$

Based on this statement, power spectral density statement of AR parameter, PSD estimation is formed as :

$$\widehat{P}_{cov} = \frac{\sigma^2}{\left|1 + \sum_{k=1}^{p} \hat{a}\,(k).\,e^{-j2\pi fk}\right|^2} \tag{4.15}$$

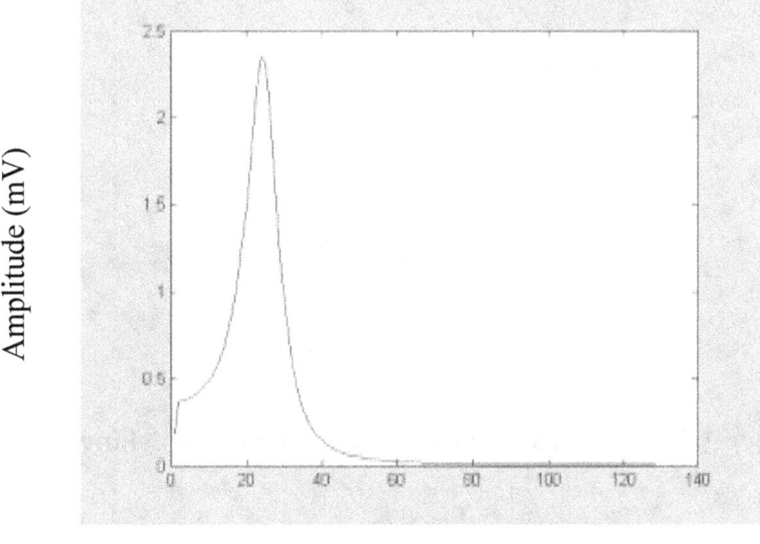

Figure 4.1 Read Task for Subject1 Using Covariance Method

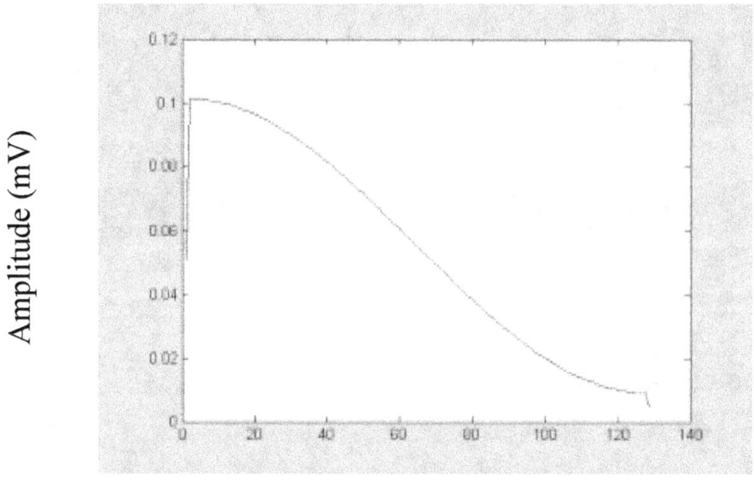

Frequency (Hz)

Figure 4.2 Relax Task for Subject1 Using Covariance Method

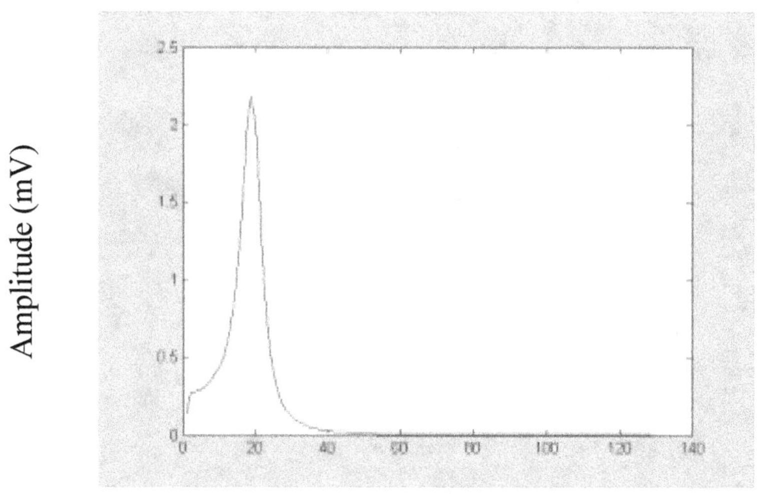

Frequency (Hz)

Figure 4.3 Maths Task for Subject1 Using Covariance Method

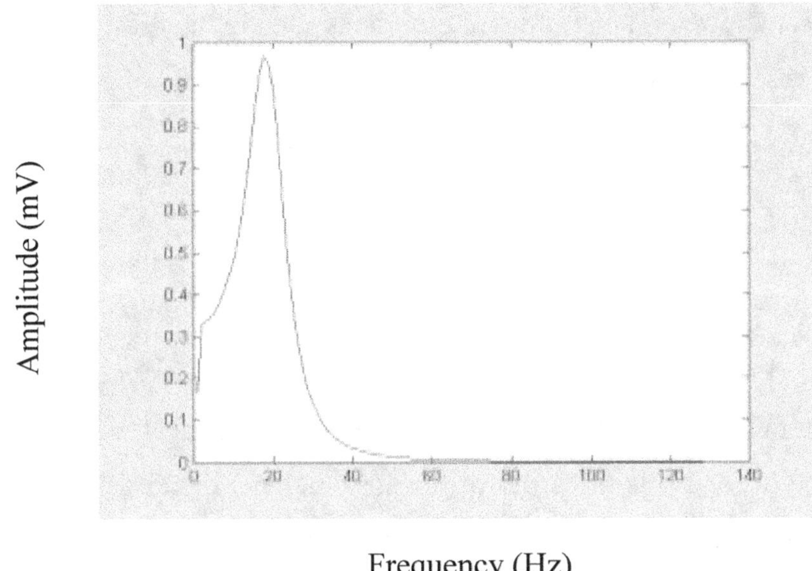

Figure 4.4 Spell Task for Subject1 Using Covariance Method

Alpha and Beta wave obtained is converted into data in which the amplitude value is in voltage. To extract the PSD features, we used Covariance algorithm. 12 and 24 features were extracted for the single channel and the two channel system respectively. It is done by using Matlab software version 7.0. These features are used to train and test the neural networks. Figure 4.1 to 4.4 shown power spectrum distribution range for read, relax, maths and spell tasks using covariance algorithm.

4.3.1.2 Burg Method

The Burg method belongs to the class of parametric methods based on AR spectral estimation is based on minimizing the forward and backward prediction errors while satisfying the Levinson-Durbin Recursion. Burg method is one of the techniques proposed by Burg in 1967 for computation of AR modeling coefficients. The Burg method does not use windowing to the data. A number of different combinations of these two parameters have been tested and a model order of 2,300 proved to be appropriate for the data length used. For this method, it is possible to determine the model order according to criteria for minimizing the noise influence. However, none of these criteria applied in the present case, will the model order determine, based on a trial and error approach.

$$x[n] = -\sum_{k=1}^{p} a_k x[n-k] + e[n] \qquad (4.9)$$

Where $x[n]$ is the observed output of the system, $e(n)$ is the unobserved input data and a_k are its coefficients. The input $e(n)$ is considered as zero mean white noise process with unknown variance σ^2, and p is the order of the system. This model is commonly referred as AR (p). The a_k coefficients are determined minimizing the forward and backward prediction errors in the least square sense. The PSD estimation is obtained from the following equation:

$$P_B(f) = \frac{E_P}{\left|1 + \sum_{k=1}^{p} a_p e^{-j2\pi f k}\right|^2} \qquad (4.10)$$

Where E_p is the total least square error of order p. The major advantages of the Burg method are its high frequency resolution, the AR model is always stable and it is computationally very efficient. It exhibits, however, several limitations such as line splitting in the PSD for low signal to noise ratio and frequency shifting from the true frequency, especially for short data record (Lawrence et al., 1987; Kay et al., 1988).

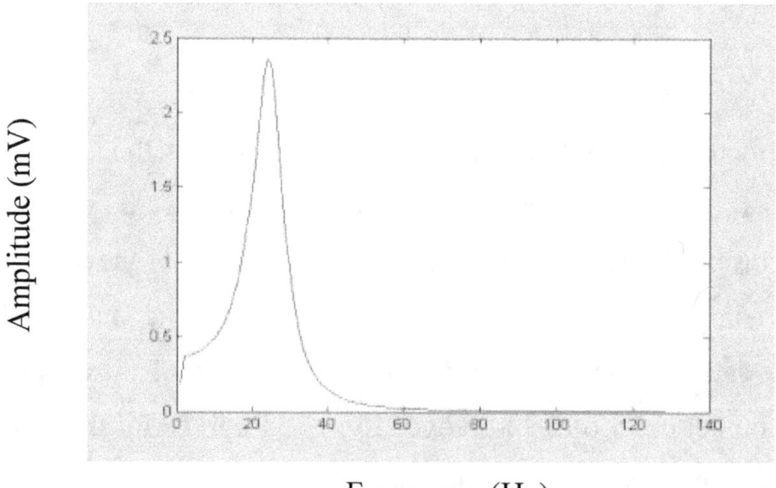

Figure 4.5 Read Task for Subject1 Using Burg Method

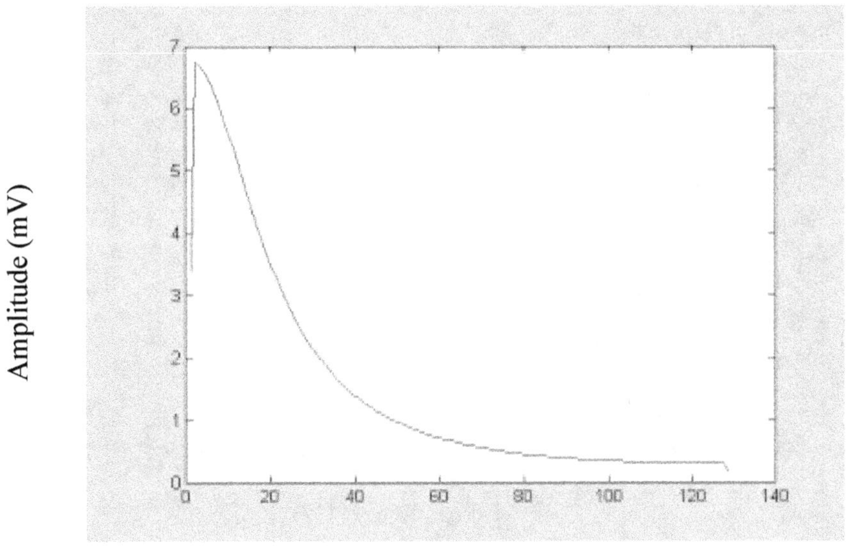

Frequency (Hz)

Figure 4.6 Relax Task for Subject1 Using Burg Method

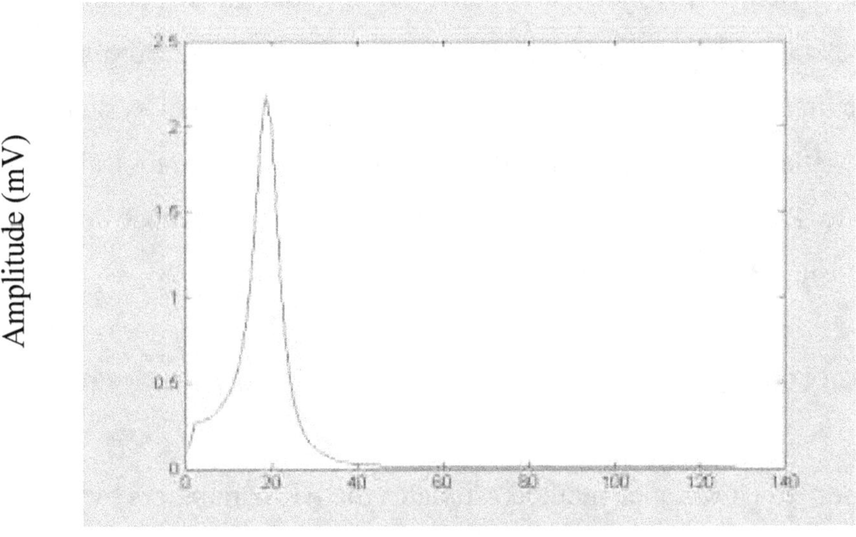

Frequency (Hz)

Figure 4.7 Maths Task for Subject1 Using Burg Method

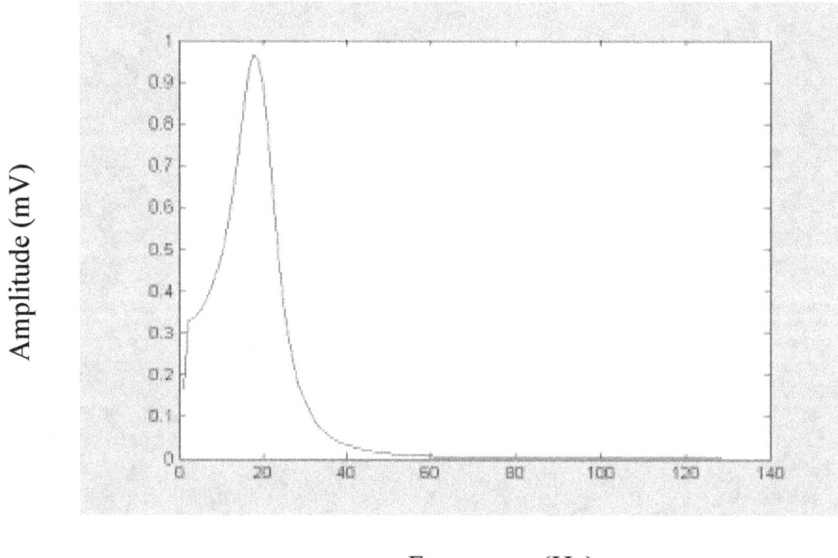

Figure 4.8 Spell Task for Subject1 Using Burg Method

Alpha and Beta wave obtained is converted into data in which the amplitude value is in voltage. To extract the power spectral density features, we used Burg algorithm. 12 and 24 features were extracted for the single channel and the two channel system respectively. It is done by using Matlab software version 7.0. These features are used to train and test the neural networks. Figure 4.5 to 4.8 shown power spectrum distribution range for read, relax, maths and spell tasks using Burg algorithm.

4.3.1.3 Modified Covariance

The Modified Covariance method estimates the AR parameters by minimizing the average of the estimated forward and backward prediction error power.

$$\widehat{h}(n) = -\sum_{k=1}^{p} a(k)h(n-k) \tag{4.16}$$

$$\hat{h}(n) = -\sum_{k=1}^{p} a^*(k)h(n+k) \tag{4.17}$$

The modified covariance for estimating the spectral content fitting an AR linear prediction filter model of a given order of signals are used. The input is a frame of consecutive time samples, which is assumed to be the output of an AR system driven by white noise (Hayes et al., 1996).

A (k) is the AR filter parameter. Modified covariance is found by a minimizing the average of the power estimations of AR parameters

$$\hat{p} = \frac{1}{2}(\hat{p}^f + \hat{p}^b) \tag{4.18}$$

Here *n* is the exemplification number

$$\hat{p}^f = \frac{1}{N-P}\sum_{n=0}^{N-1}\left| h(n) + \sum_{k=1}^{p} a(k)h(n-k)\right| 2 \tag{4.19}$$

$$\hat{p}^b = \frac{1}{N-P}\sum_{n=0}^{N-1-P}\left| h(n) + \sum_{k=1}^{p} a^*(k)h(n+k)\right| 2 \tag{4.20}$$

PSD can be acquired by using values of *a (k)* in between *k=1, 2,...,p*. Estimation of white noise variance is acquired with this statement.

$$\hat{\tau}^2 = chh(0,0) + \sum_{k=1}^{p} \hat{a}(k)chh(0,k) \tag{4.21}$$

PSD is acquired with the mathematical statement in the below

$$phh(f) = \frac{\tau^2}{\left|1 + \sum_{k=1}^{p} \hat{a}(k).e^{-j2\pi fk}\right| 2} \tag{4.22}$$

The difference between the modified covariance and covariance technique is the definition of the autocorrelation estimator. Based on the estimates of the AR parameters, PSD prediction is expressed as follows:

$$\hat{p}_{mcov}(f) = \frac{\hat{\sigma}^2}{\left|1 + \sum_{k=1}^{p} \hat{a}(k) e^{-j2\pi fk}\right|^2}$$

(4.23)

The advantages of the modified covariance method for estimating the parameters of the AR model are yields statistically stable spectral estimates with high frequency resolution.

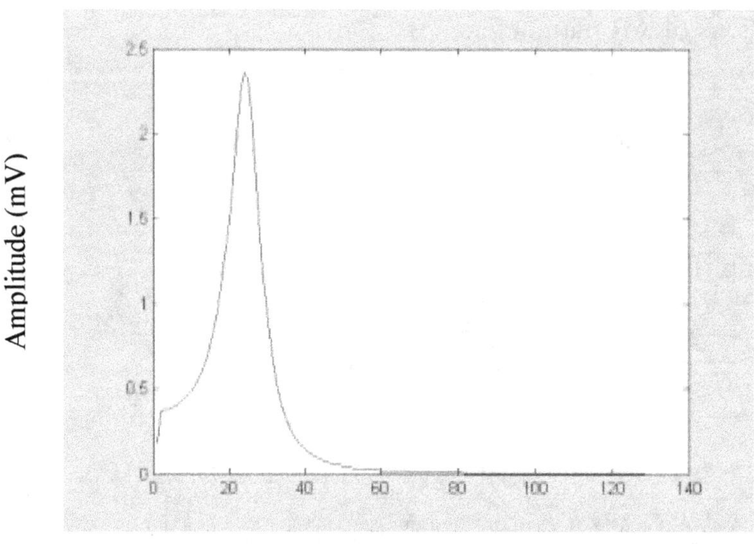

Figure 4.9 Read Task for Subject1 Using Modified Covariance Method

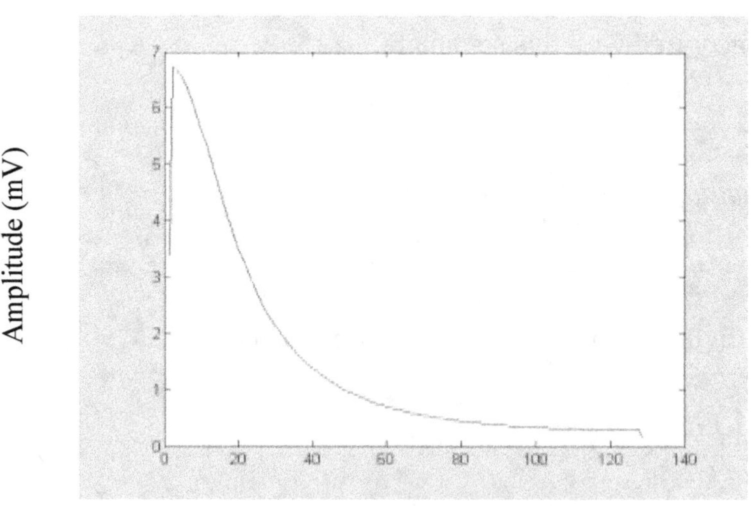

Figure 4.10 Relax Task for Subject1 Using Modified Covariance Method

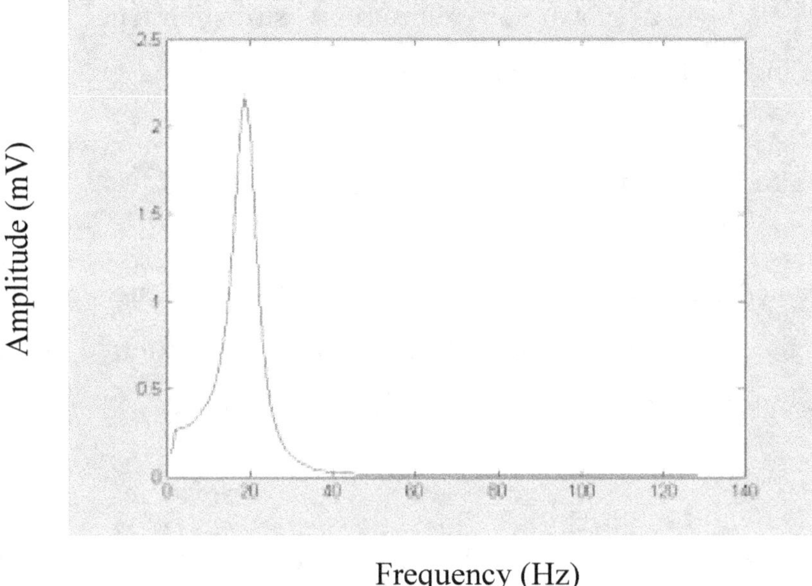

Figure 4.11 Maths Task for Subject1 Using Modified Covariance method

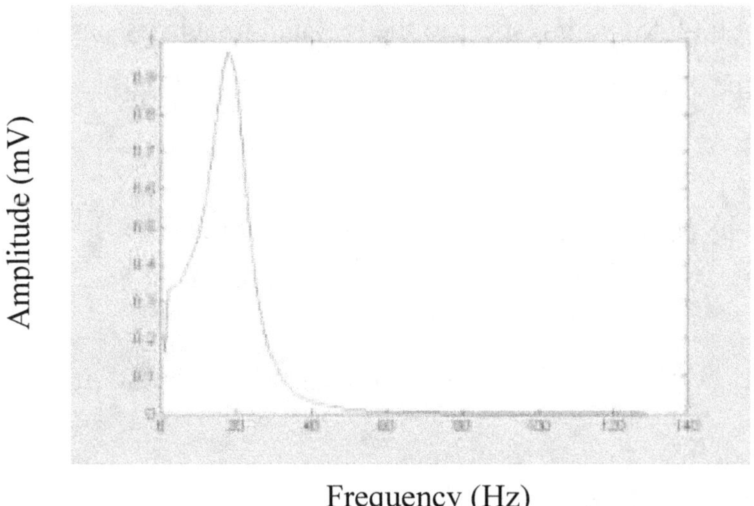

Figure 4.12 Spell Task for Subject1 Using Modified Covariance Method

Alpha and Beta wave obtained is converted into data which the amplitude value is in voltage. To extract the power spectral density features, we used Modified Covariance algorithm. 12 and 24 features were extracted for single channel and two channel system respectively. It is done by using Matlab software version 7.0. These features are used to train and test in neural networks. Figure 4.8 to 4.12 shown power spectrum distribution range for read, relax, maths and spell tasks using Modified Covariance.

4.3.1.4 Yule–Walker Method

It is assumed that the data $\{x(0), x(1), \dots \dots, x(N-1)\}$ are observed. In the Yule-Walker method, the autocorrelation methods as it is sometimes referred to the AR parameters are estimated by minimizing an estimate of prediction error power.

$$variance = p = \frac{1}{N} \sum_{n=-\infty}^{\infty} \left| x(n) + \sum_{k=1}^{p} a(k)x(n-k) \right|^2 \qquad (4.24)$$

The samples of the $x(n)$ process which is not observed (i.e., those not in the range $0 \leq n \leq N\text{-}1$) is set equal to zero in Eq.(4.25). The estimated prediction error power is minimized by differentiating Eq.(4.25) with respect to the real and imaginary parts of the $a\,(k)$. This may be done by using the complex gradient to yield (Hayes et al., 1996).

$$\frac{1}{N} \sum_{n=-\infty}^{\infty} \left(x(n) + \sum_{k=1}^{p} a(k)x(n-k) \right) x^*(n-1) = 0 \qquad (4.25)$$

With: $l=1,2,\dots\dots\dots,p$. This set of equation in terms of autocorrelation function estimates becomes:

$$r_p + R_p a = 0 \qquad (4.26)$$

Where

$$r(k) = \begin{cases} \dfrac{1}{N} \displaystyle\sum_{n-0}^{N-1-k} x^*(n)x(n+K), & k = 0,1,\dots\dots p \\ r^*(-k), & k = (-p+1), (-p+2), \dots, -1 \end{cases} \qquad (4.27)$$

From Eq.(4.30) the are parameter estimates are found as:

$$a = -R_p^{-1}r_p \tag{4.28}$$

The estimate of the white noise variance σ2 is calculated as:

$$\sigma^2 = r(0) + \sum_{k=1}^{p} a(k)(-k) \tag{4.29}$$

From the estimates of the auto regressive parameters, PSD estimation is given as:

$$p(f) = \frac{\sigma^2}{\left|1 + \sum_{k=1}^{p} a(k)e^{-j2\pi fk}\right|^2} \tag{4.30}$$

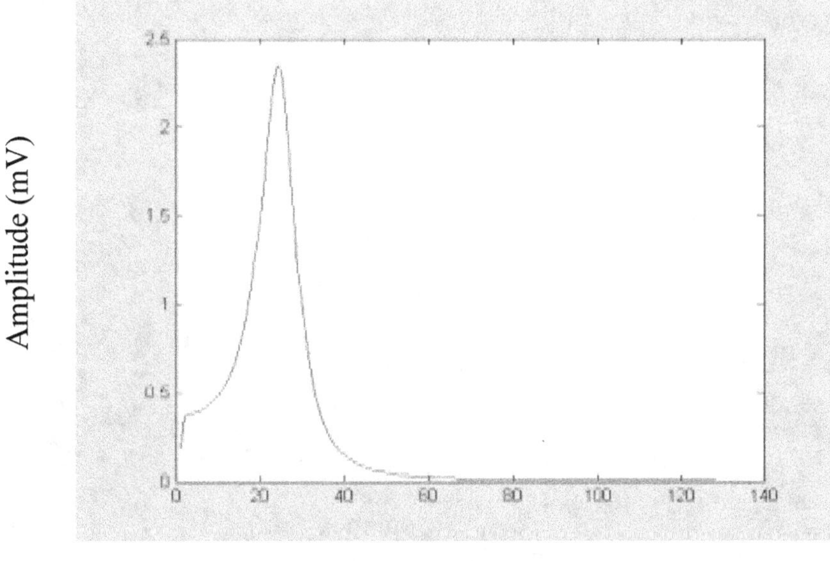

Figure 4.13 Read Task for Subject1 Using Yule–Walker Method

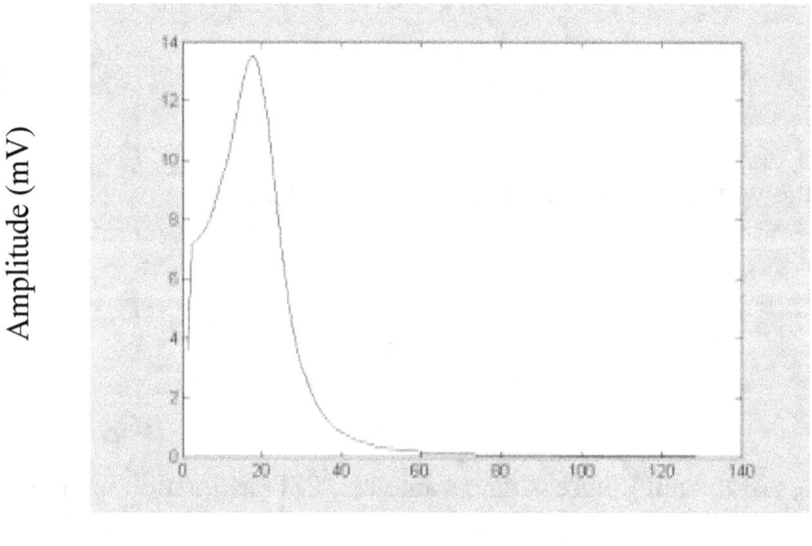

Figure 4.14 Relax Task for Subject1 Using Yule–Walker Method

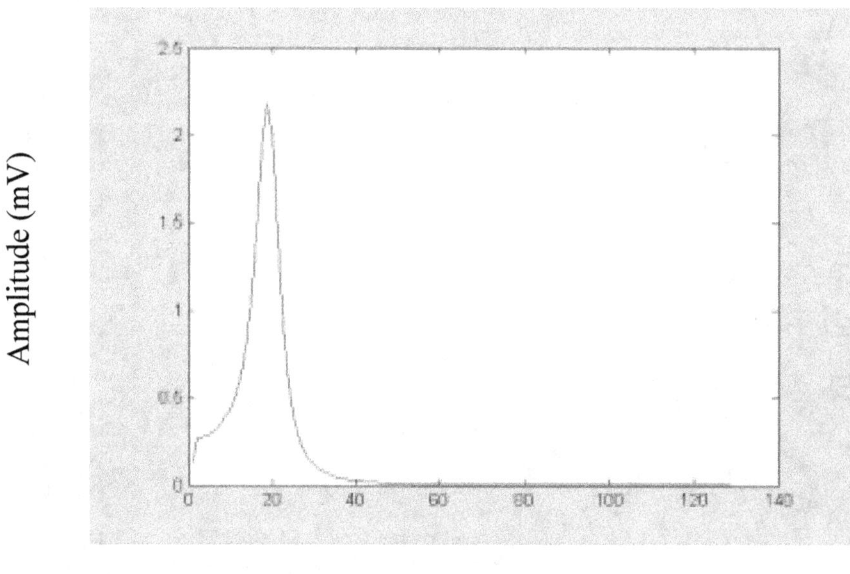

Figure 4.15 Maths Task for Subject1 Using Yule–Walker Method

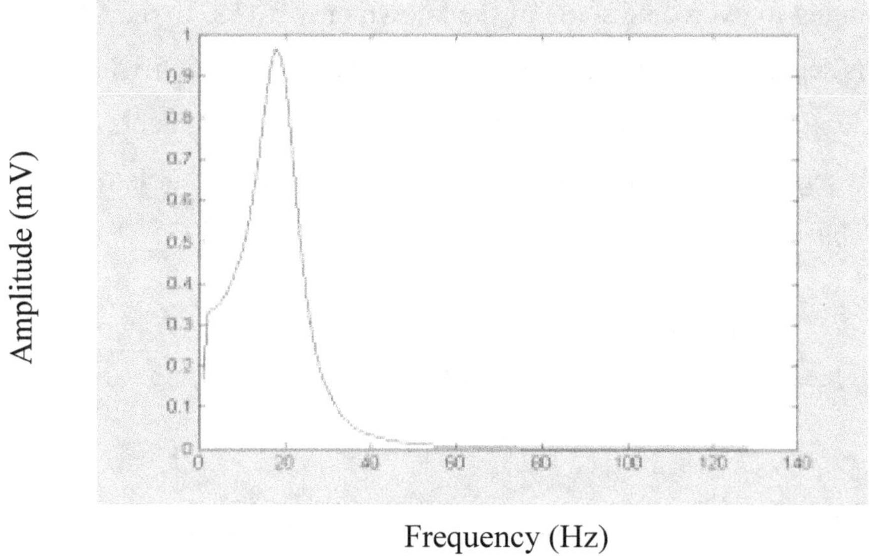

Figure 4.16 Spell Task for Subject1 Using Yule–Walker Method

Alpha and Beta wave obtained is converted into data in which the amplitude value is in voltage. To extract the power spectral density features, we used Yule–Walker algorithm. 12 and 24 features were extracted for the single channel and the two channel system respectively. It is done by using Matlab software version 7.0. These features are used to train and test the neural networks. From the Figure 4.13 to 4.16 shown power spectrum distribution range for read, relax, maths and spell tasks using Yule -Walker algorithm.

4.3.2 Non-Parametric Methods

The simple and easy, non-parametric methods do not assume a fixed structure of a model. It can expand to accommodate the complexity of data. It is based on fewer assumptions like wide sense stationary; hence their applicability is much wider than parametric methods.

4.3.2.1 Welch Method

Welch spectral prediction is a method based on Fast Fourier Transform. The Welch method is also a nonparametric method and it is based on some modification of the

Periodogram aiming to overcome some of the known drawbacks. In the Welch algorithm, the input signal x is segmented into eight sections of equal length, each with 50% overlap. Any remaining entries in x that cannot be included in the eight segments of equal length are discarded. Each segment is windowed with a hamming window that is of the same length as the segment (Subha et al., 2010; Proakis et al., 1996).

$$P_{REF} = \left| \frac{1}{N} \sum_{N=1}^{N} X(n)\exp(-2\pi f) \right| \tag{4.31}$$

The prediction of power spectral density with Welch method is expressed as follows

$$\hat{p}welch(f)" = \frac{1}{L} \sum_{t=0}^{L-1} \hat{s}\,xx(f) \tag{4.32}$$

L is the length of the time series. Examining the short data registries with conjoint and non rectangular window reduces the predictive resolution. The Welch method also obtains a better resolution than Periodogram if the signal noise level is low (Subha et al., 2010; Proakis et al., 1996).

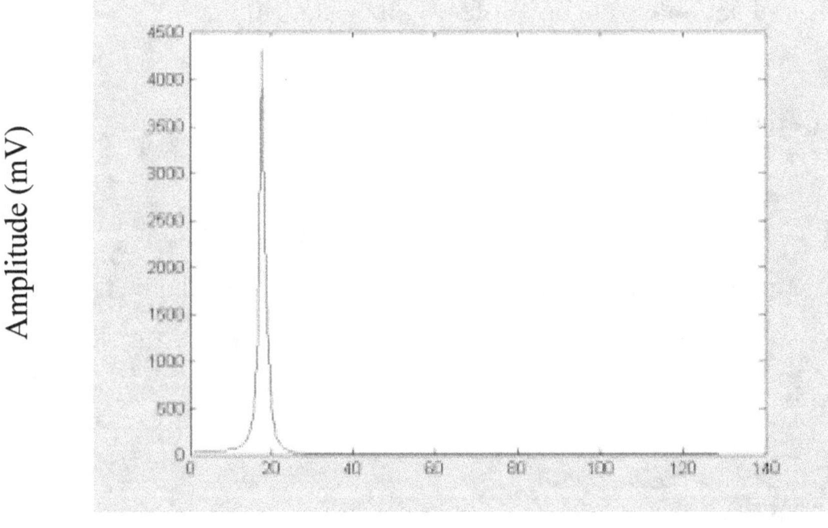

Frequency (Hz)

Figure 4.17 Read Task for Subject1 Using Welch Method

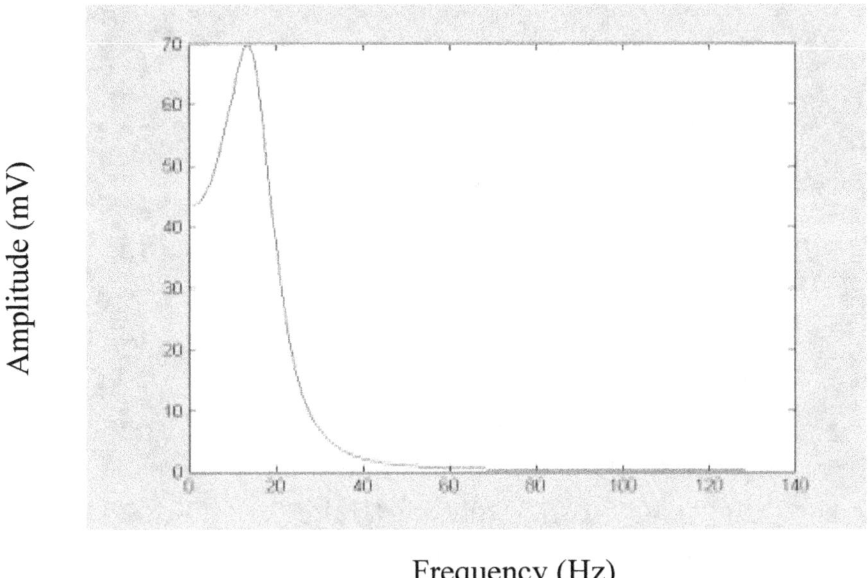

Figure 4.18 Relax Task for Subject1 Using Welch Method

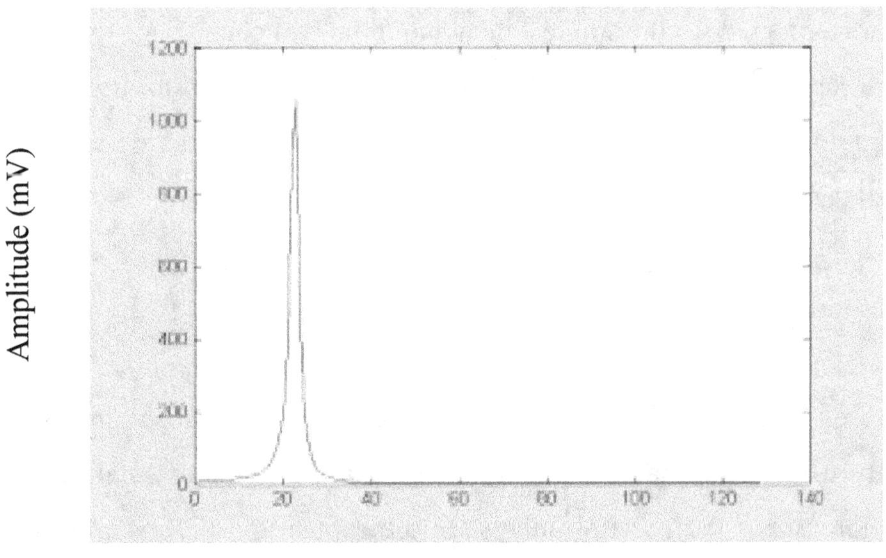

Figure 4.19 Maths Task for Subject1 Using Welch Method

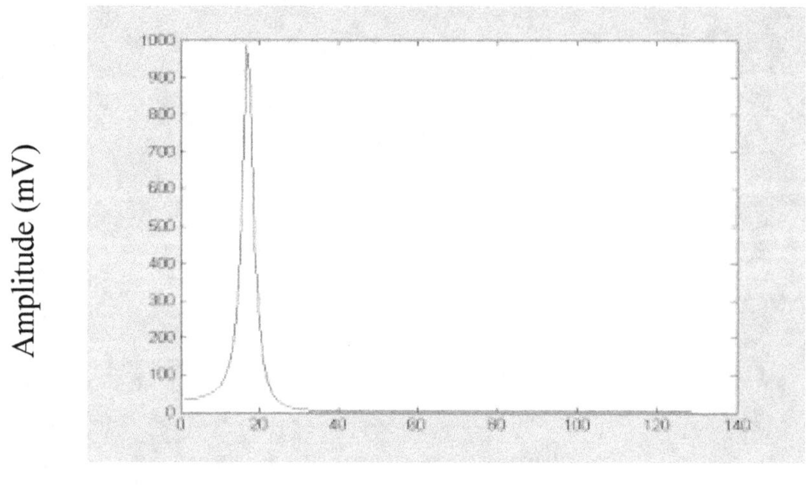

Frequency (Hz)

Figure 4.20 Spell Task for Subject1 Using Welch Method

Alpha and Beta wave obtained is converted into data in which the amplitude value is in voltage. To extract the Power Spectral Density features, we used Welch algorithm. 12 and 24 features were extracted for the single channel and the two channel system respectively. It is done by using Matlab software version 7.0. These features are used to train and test in neural networks. From Figure 4.17 to 4.20 shown power spectrum distribution range for read, relax, maths and spell tasks using Welch algorithm.

4.3.3 High Resolution Method

High resolution methods aim to separate the observation space in a signal subspace, containing only useful information, and its orthogonal complement, called noise subspace. This composition makes the spectral analysis more robust and highly improves the spectral resolution.

4.3.3.1 Multiple Signal Classification

The MUSIC method belongs to the class of Eigen decomposition methods for which the observed data can be represented by P complex sinusoids in white noise, as follows

$$x[n] = -\sum_{i=1}^{p} A_i\, e^{j2\pi f i n} + e[n] \qquad (4.33)$$

In (4.33), A_i is the complex amplitude of the i-th complex sinusoid, f_i is its frequency, and $e(n)$ is the zero mean white noise in the input $x(n)$. This method uses the eigenvector decomposition of the input signal to obtain two orthogonal subspaces. The p largest Eigenvalues span the signal subspace with dimension p. The remaining Eigenvalues span the noise subspace with the dimension $(M\text{-}p)$, M being the dimension of the estimated autocorrelation matrix. From the orthogonality condition of both subspaces, the pseudo spectrum can be obtained using the following frequency estimator:

$$P_B(f) = \frac{1}{\sum_{l=P+1}^{M}|s(f)^H V^K|^2} \qquad (4.34)$$

Where V_K is the noise eigenvector and $s(f)$ is the signal vector is given as:

$$s(f) = \begin{bmatrix} 1 & e^{j2\pi f} e^{j4\pi f} & \dots\dots e^{j2\pi f(N-1)} \end{bmatrix} \qquad (4.35)$$

It must be noted that the pseudo spectrum is not a true PSD estimator, it is used for locating the frequencies contained in the signal, as sharp peaks appear *for f=fi*. After the determination of the p frequencies, the true power density estimates for the P sinusoids can be performed using the autocorrelation matrix (Lawrence et al., 1987; Kay et al., 1988).

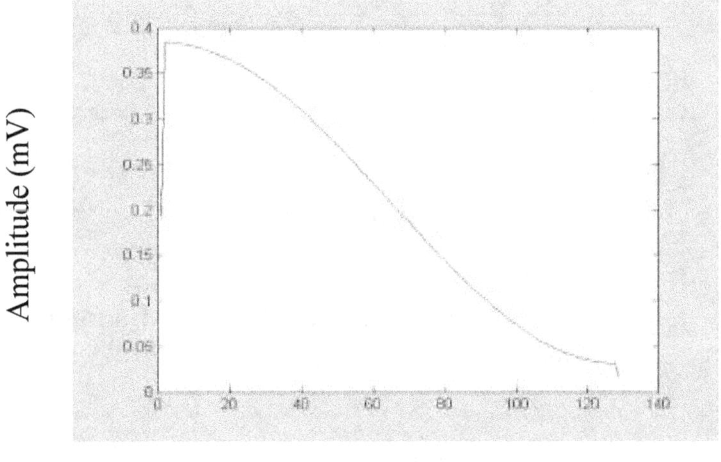

Figure 4.21 Read Task for Subject1 Using MUSIC Method

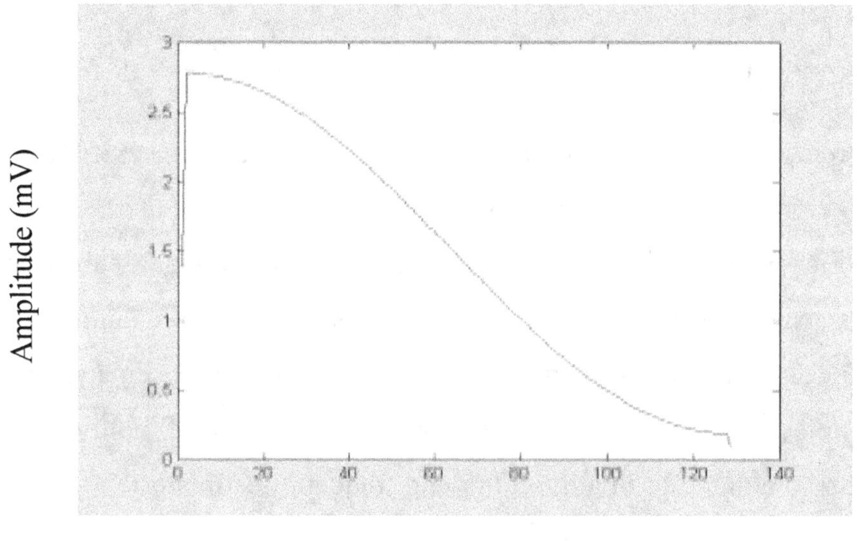

Figure 4.22 Relax Task for Subject1 Using MUSIC Method

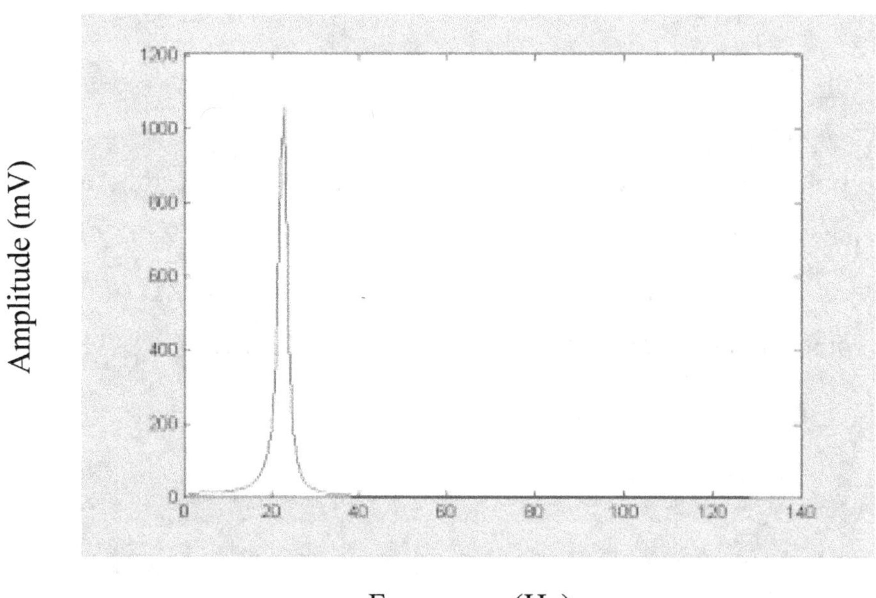

Figure 4.23 Maths Task for Subject1 Using MUSIC Method

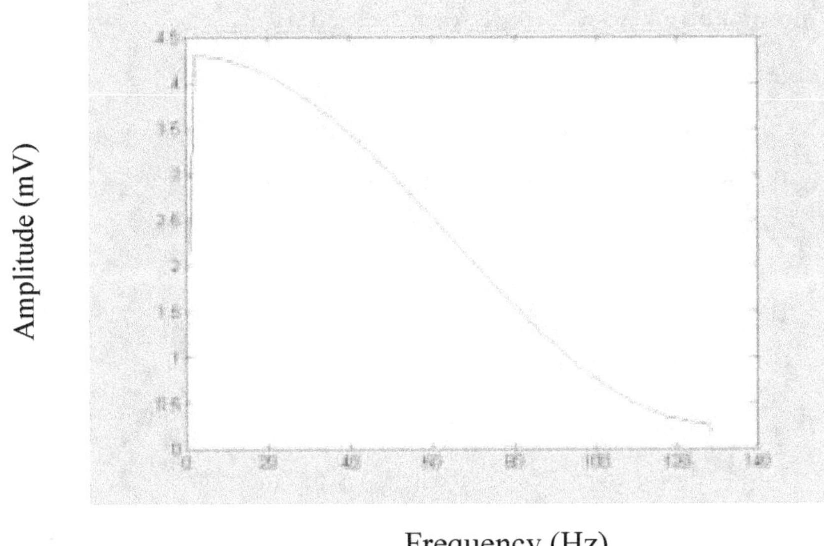

Figure 4.24 Spell Task for Subject1 Using MUSIC Method

Alpha and Beta wave obtained is converted into data in which the amplitude value is in voltage. To extract the PSD features, we used MUSIC algorithm. 12 and 24 features were extracted for the single channel and the two channel system respectively. It is done by using Matlab software version 7.0. These features are used to train and test in neural networks. Figure 4.21 to 4.24 power spectrum distribution range for read, relax, maths and spell tasks using MUSIC algorithm.

4.4 ARTIFICIAL NEURAL NETWORKS

Artificial Neural Networks (ANN) are composed of interconnecting artificial neurons. Artificial neural networks may either be used to gain an understanding of biological neural networks, or for solving artificial intelligence problems without necessarily creating a model of a real biological system. The real, biological nervous system is highly complex and a very flexible system. Adaptive nature is the important feature of artificial neural network. An artificial neural network is a mathematical function conceived as a simple model of real biological neurons. This is a simplified model of real neurons known a threshold logic unit.

- ❖ The input neurons arrive in the form of signal
- ❖ The signals build up in the cells
- ❖ Finally the cell discharge through output
- ❖ The cell can start building up a real neuron is shown in Figure 4.25.

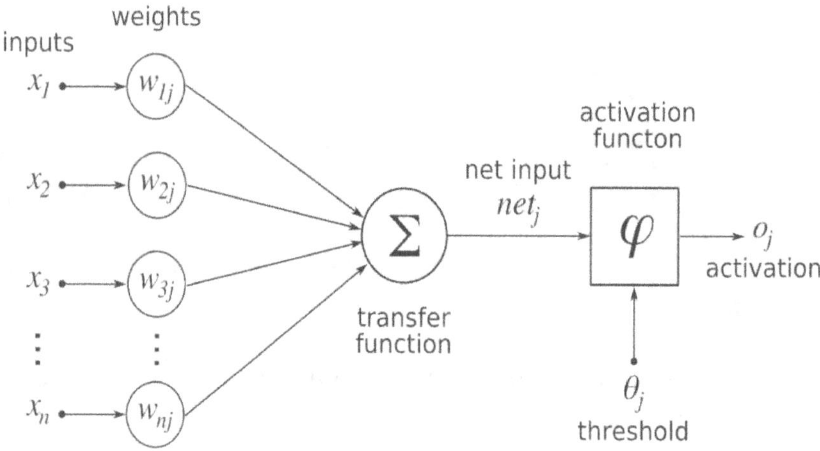

Figure 4.25 Artificial Neuron with Activation Function

There are three layers consists in a network such as namely input layer output layer and hidden layers. In input layer, the neurons receive the external input signal and perform no computation, but simply transfer the input signal to neurons to another layer. Neurons in the hidden layer detect the feature; the weight of the neurons represents the feature the hidden in input patterns. These features are presented to the output layer for determining the output pattern. With one hidden layer, we can represent any continuous function can be represented. The neurons in output layer receive signal from neurons either in the input layer or hidden layer (Yasrebi et al., 2008).

The most important characteristic of an artificial neural network is its ability to learn. Learning is a process in which the network adjusts its parameters the (synaptic weights) in response to input stimuli so that the actual output response converges to the desired output response converges to the desired output response. When the actual output response in the same as the desired one, the network has completed the learning phase and the network has acquired knowledge. Learning or training categorized into supervised,unsupervised and reinforced training. The supervised training is commonly used.

Supervised training requires the pairing of each input vector with a target vector representing the desired output. During the training session an input vector is applied to the network, and its result response differs from the target response, the network generates an error signal. The error signal is then used to calculate the adjustment that should be made in the synaptic weights so that the actual output matches the target output. The error minimization in this kind of training requires a supervisor or teacher, hence the name supervised training.

Unsupervised training is employed in self organizing neural net. In contrast to supervised learning,it does not require a teacher. In this method of training the input vector similar type of grouped without the use of training, the input vector of similar types of grouped without the use of training data to specific how a typical member of each group looks. During this training the neural network receives the input pattern and organizes this pattern into categories. Even though unsupervised training does not require a teacher, it requires certain guidelines to form groups based on color, shape or any other properties. Meanwhile reinforced training,it is similar to supervised training. In this method, the teacher does not indicate how close the actual output to the desired output is, but yields only pass or fail indication. Thus, the error generated during reinforced training is binary.

4.5 CLASSIFICATION USING NEURAL NETWORK

ANN Classification is an example of supervised learning. Multilayer networks are applied with success to determine different issues by training them in a supervised manner with an extreme algorithmic rule called back-propagation algorithmic rule. ANN classification is the process of learning to separate samples into different classes by finding common features between samples of known classes. Making guesses on unknown samples is regularly a way of testing the ANN classifier. Two types of samples have used to distinguish samples, one is called testing samples and other is training samples. The performance of ANN algorithm was accessed by following measures;

❖ **True Positive (TP)**

The ANN identifies an input signal exactly, classifying and labeling the signal correctly.

$$TPR = \frac{TP}{P} \tag{4.36}$$

Positive= (True Positive + False Positive)

❖ **True Negative (TN)**

The ANN identifies an input signal exactly, classifying and labeling the signal differently.

$$TNR = \frac{TN}{N} \tag{4.37}$$

Negative= (True Negative +False Negative)

❖ **False Positive (FP)**

The ANN identifies a different input signal, classifying and labeling the signal correctly.

$$FN = \frac{FP}{(FP + TN)} \tag{4.38}$$

❖ **False Negative (FN)**

The ANN identifies a different input signal, classifying and labeling the signal differently.

$$FN = \frac{FN}{(TP + FN)} \tag{4.39}$$

❖ **Sensitivity (SE)**

The ability of the classifier to detect the exact EEG signals. Number of True Positive (TP) results divided by sum of True Positive (TN) and False Negative (FN) are expressed in percentage

$$SE = \frac{TP}{(TP + FN)} * 100 \tag{4.40}$$

❖ **Specificity (SE)**

The ability of the classifier to detect the different brain signals. Specificity of a test refers to the possibility that test results will be negative among subject whose EEG signals are not clear. Number of True Negative (TN) results divided by sum of True Negative (TN) and False Negative (FN) are expressed in percentage

$$SE = \frac{TN}{(TN + FN)} * 100 \tag{4.41}$$

❖ **Positive Productivity (PD)**

Number of True Positive (TP) results divided by sum of True Positive and False Positive (FP) results are expressed in percentage

$$Positive\ Predictivity = \frac{TP}{(TP + FP)} * 100 \tag{4.42}$$

4.6 STEPS IN DESIGNING THE NEURAL NETWORK

Design and development of neural networks for classification purpose consist of the following steps are:

4.6.1 Data Set Pre-Processing

Features extracted from the EEG signals must be pre processed to provide feature values in the proper range.

4.6.2 Training and Testing the Sets

Common observation is to divide the time series into three different sets, training, testing and validation sets. The training set is the largest set and it is used by the neural network to learn the patterns in the data. The testing set ranging in the size from 10% to 30% of the training set is used to evaluate the generalization ability of the supposedly trained network. The network that performs best on the training set is chosen for the real time testing. The ratio between the training and testing sets chosen in our experiment varies from 80%:20%.

4.6.3 Number of Hidden Layers

Hidden layer provides the network with its ability to generalize. Within the neural network one hidden layer with sufficient number of hidden neurons is capable of approximate any continuous function. In practice a neural network with three hidden layers are widely used and have performed well. Increasing the number of hidden layers also increases the computational time and danger of over fitting which leads to out-of-sample recognition performance. The FFNN used in this research is designed with one hidden layer.

4.6.4 Number of Hidden Neurons

It is necessary to notice that the rules which calculate the amount of hidden neurons as a multiple number of input neurons implicitly assume that the training set is at least twice as large as the number of weights and preferably four or more times as large. If it is not case then the thumb case can quickly lead to the over fitted models since the hidden neurons are directly dependent upon the input neurons. The solution is either increase the size of the training set or to a set an upper limit on the number of input neurons so that the number of weights is at least half the number of training facts. Selecting the number of best hidden neurons involves experimentation. The three hidden neurons for FFNN are chosen experimentally, depending upon the features selected.

4.6.5 Number of Output Neurons

Deciding the number of output neurons is somewhat more straightforward depending on the number of classifications. In this research, five and three output neurons are used in the FFNN models using single channel and two channels respectively.

4.6.6 Transfer Functions

The transfer function is mathematical formulas that determine the output of a processing neuron. They are referred as transformation. The purpose of training function is to prevent output from reaching very large values which can paralyze neural networks and their training. The sigmoid transfer function is chosen for the FFNN as the input and output sets.

4.6.7 Evaluation Criteria

The most common function utilized in NN is the sum of the squared errors. Other error functions offered by software vendors include least absolute deviations, least fourth power, asymmetric least squares and percentage difference.

4.6.8 Neural Network Training

Training a NN to learn the patterns in the data involves iteratively presenting it with examples of correct answers; the objective of the training is to set the weights between the neurons that determine the global minimum of the error function. Unless the model is over fitted, this set of weights should provide good generalization. The FFNN neural network is trained using the Back Propagation training algorithm.

4.6.9 Number of Training Iterations

In this approach to training is stopped only if there is no improvement in the error function based on a reasonable number of selected starting weights. Training is stopped after a predetermined number of iterations and the network's ability to generalize on the testing set is evaluated and training is resumed.

4.6.10 Neural Network Models

Neural networks have been successfully used in a variety of medical applications. Recent advances in the field of neural networks have made them attractive for analyzing signals. The application of neural networks has opened a new area for solving problems not resolvable by other signal processing techniques. In contrast to the conventional spectral analysis methods, ANNs not only model the signal, but also make a decision as to the class of signal. Another advantage of ANN analysis over existing methods of biomedical signal analysis is that, after an ANN has trained satisfactorily and the values of the weights and biases have been stored, testing and subsequent implementation is rapid. During implementation of the combined neural networks the predictions of the networks in the first-level were combined with second-level neural network. The results of the present study showed that significant improvement is achieved with accuracy by applying neural networks as the second-level model compared to the stand-alone multilayer perception.

4.7 FEED FORWARD NEURAL NETWORK BASED CLASSIFIER

Feed-forward neural network (FFNN), which is shown in Figure 4.26 one of the most common and first developed types of ANN. Back propagation algorithm resembles multilayer Feed Forward Network. The errors propagate backwards from output nodes to the input nodes. Network activation flow in one direction only, from the input layer to output layer passing through the hidden layer. Each unit is connected in the forward direction to every unit in the next layer. It is a multilayer feed forward network with one layer of hidden units. The input layer is connected to hidden layer and output layer is connected by means of interconnection weights. The bias is provided for both hidden and output layer to act upon the net input. Mathematical formula used an algorithm can be applied to any network which is the advantage of using BPN (Bishop et al., 1995). The architecture of the FFNN is shown in Figure 4.26.

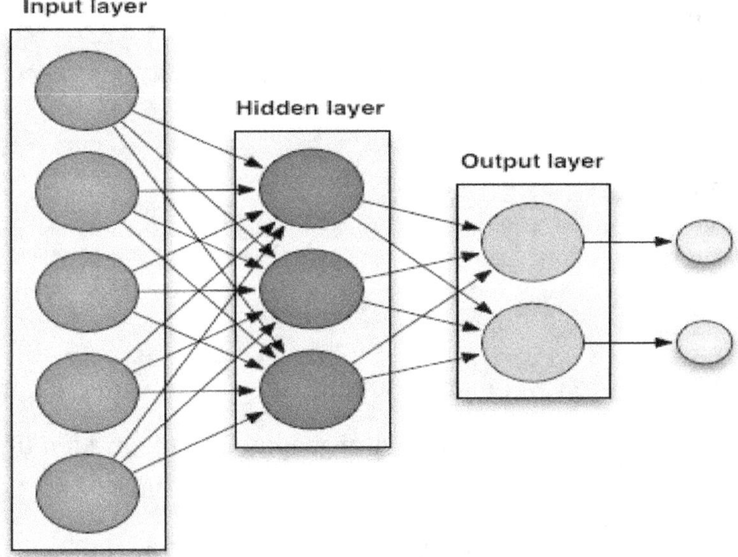

Figure 4.26 Architecture of Feed Forward Neural Network

4.7.1 BackPropagation Learning Method

The most widely used neural-network learning method is the BP algorithm. This backpropagation algorithm can easily train a neural network. Learning in a neural network involves modifying the weights and biases of the network in order to minimize a cost function. The cost function always includes an error term a measure of how close the network's predictions are to the class labels for the examples in the training set. Additionally, it may include a complexity term that reacts a prior distribution over the values that the parameters can take.

The activation function considered for each node in the network is the binary sigmoid function defined by s = 1 as output = 1/1+e-x, where x is the sum of the weighted inputs to that particular node. This is a common function used in many FFNN. This function limits the output of all nodes in the network to be between 0 and 1. Note all neural networks are basically trained until the error for each training iteration stopped decreasing. Noise FFNN models were developed and trained and tested with the band power features. The back propagation training algorithm involves three stages (Sivanandam et al., 2003) the feed forward of the input training pattern, the calculation and back propagation of the associated weight error and the weight adjustments. The training algorithm is shown below

x : input training vector

$$X = x_1, x_2, \ldots, x_i, \ldots, x_n.$$

t : Output target vector

$$t = t_1, t_2, \ldots, t_j, \ldots, t_m.$$

δ : Portion of error correction weight adjustment for w_{jk} that is due to an error at the output unit Y_k, which is back propagated to the hidden units that feed into Y_k.

δj : Portion of error correction weight adjustments for v_{ij} that is due to the back propagation of error to the hidden unit , Z_j.

α : Learning rate.

X_i : i^{th} input unit.

v_{oj} : Bias on j^{th} hidden unit.

Net input to Z_j,

$$z_{inj} = v_{oj} + \Sigma \, i \, x_i v_{ij}$$

And

$$z_j = f z_{inj}$$

If w_{ok} is the bias on k^{th} output unit and Y_k is the kth output unit. Then the net input to Y_k

$$y_{ink} = w_{ok} + \Sigma j \, z_j \, w_{jk}$$

And

$$y_k = f y_{ink}$$

STEP1: Initialize the weights.

STEP2: While stopping condition is false, do steps 3 to 10.

STEP3: For each training pair x:t, do steps 4 to 9

STEP4: Each input unit X_i, i=1, 2… n receives the input signal, x_i and broadcasts it to the next layer.

STEP5: For each hidden layer neuron denoted as Z_j, j=1,2, …,p.

$$z_{inj} = v_{oj} + \Sigma i \, x_i \, v_{ij}$$

$$z_j = f z_{inj}$$

Braodcast z_j to the next layer.

STEP6: For each output neuron Y_k, k =1, 2,…,m

$$y_{ink} = w_{ok} + \Sigma j z_j w_{jk}$$

$$y_k = f y_{ink}$$

STEP7: Compute δ_k for each output neuron, Y_k.

$$\delta_k = t_k - y_k f' y_{ink}$$

$$\Delta w_{jk} = \alpha \delta_k z_j$$

$$\Delta w_{ok} = \alpha \delta_k, \text{ since } z_0 = 1$$

STEP8: For each hidden neuron

$$\delta_{inj} = \Sigma k = 1m \; \delta_k w_{jk} \quad j = 1,2,…,p$$

$$\delta_j = \delta_{inj} \, f' z_{inj}$$

$$\Delta v_{ij} = \alpha \delta_j \, x_i$$

$$\Delta v_{oj} - \alpha \delta_j$$

STEP9: Update weights

$$w_{jk} \text{new} = w_{jk} \text{old} + \Delta w_{jk}$$

$$v_{ij} \text{new} = v_{ij} \text{old} + \Delta v_{ij}$$

STEP10: Test for stopping condition.

The FFNN is trained using Levenberg Back Propagation training algorithm because it finds a solution even if it starts very far off the final minimum. The network is modeled with 9 hidden neurons, which is usually determined by a number of trial and error method runs. 75% of the data is used for training and 100% data are used for testing the network model for both single and double channel systems. The FFNN is modeled using 12 and 24 input neurons for single channel and two channel system. Respectively five and four output neurons for single channel and two channel system are used to verify the individuals. The learning rate is chosen as 0.0001. Training is conducted until the average error falls below 0.001 or reaches maximum iteration limit of 1000 and testing error tolerance is fixed at 0.5.

4.8 RECURRENT NEURAL NETWORK

The ANN architecture that we explore for modeling and classifying EEG is the Recurrent Neural Network (RNN) are shown in Figure 4.27. RNN were originally developed by Jeffrey Elman in 1990 for finding patterns in natural language and have since been successfully applied to a number of practical problems. In addition to their history of successful application, RNN are appealing because it has been demonstrated that they are universal approximates of finite state machines 36.

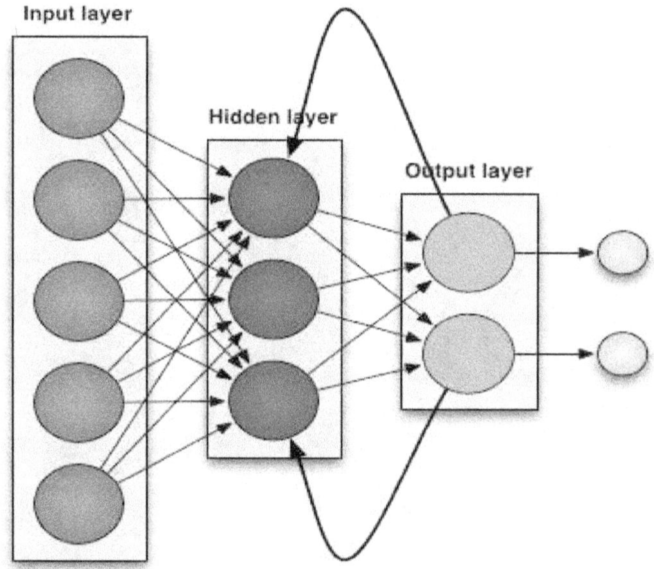

Figure 4.27 Architecture of Recurrent Neural Network

In other words, any given finite state machine can be simulated by some RNN given enough hidden units and the proper connection weights. An RNN consists of two distinct layers. The first layer, referred to as the hidden layer, is composed of a number of neurons with sigmoidal activation functions. The number of neurons in the hidden layer, also referred to as hidden units, is a parameter given during the construction of an ERNN. Each hidden unit has full incoming connections from each input as well as a constant bias value of one. Additionally, each hidden unit has full recurrent connections between every other hidden unit with a Single time step delay. In other words, the current value of each network input and the output of every hidden unit in the previous time step are fed into each hidden unit at the current time step.

The values stored in the delay lines of the recurrent connections of an RNN fully represent the state of the network at any given time. As such, we refer to these values as the context of the network. As is common practice, the initial context of our RNN is set to the zero vectors with the assumption that the network will sufficiently acclimate to the input signal and achieve an acceptable context after some initial transient period. The second layer, referred to as the visible layer, consists of one neuron per output. Each neuron in the visible layer, also referred to as a visible unit, is strictly linear, i.e., the output of each visible unit is a weighted sum of the outputs of the hidden units and a constant bias value of one. In order to formalize the RNN architecture, let us begin by defining the following constant

L: the number of network input

M: the number of hidden units

N: the number of network outputs

Next, let xt be the L $\times$ 1 vector of inputs to our network at time t and zt be the M $\times$ 1 output of our hidden layer at time t. Also, let xt be xt with a constant one appended and $\bar{z}t$ be zt with a constant one appended to our bias values. Then the output of our hidden layer at time t can be defined by the following recurrence relation

$$Z(t) = \varphi\big(H\bar{x}(t) + Sz(t-1)\big) \qquad (4.43)$$

Where H is the M × L + 1 matrix of feed forward weights in the hidden layer, S is the M ×M matrix of recurrent weights in the hidden layer and φ is our choice of sigmoid. Note that we define our initial context z0 = 0 as discussed earlier. Finally, the output of our visible layer at time t can be defined as

$$y(t) = V\bar{z}(t) \tag{4.44}$$

Where V is the N × M + 1 weight matrix for our visible layer. For the sake of notational 22 brevity, we denote the output of an ERNN at time t as

$$y(t) = emn(x(t)) \tag{4.45}$$

The RNN with one single hidden layer is trained to identify the Figure 4.27 shown the architecture of the RNN. The RNN is trained using Gradient Descent Back Propagation algorithm because it finds a solution even if it starts very far off the final minimum. The network is modeled with 9 hidden neurons, which is chosen based on trial and error method. 75% of the data is used for training and 100% data are used for testing the network model for both single and double channel systems. The RNN is modeled using 12 and 24 input neurons for single channel and two channel system. Respectively five and four output neurons for single and two channel system are used to verify the individuals. The learning rate is chosen as 0.0001. Training is conducted until the average error falls below 0.001 or reaches maximum iteration limit of 1000 and testing error tolerance is fixed at 0.5.

4.9 DESIGN OF GRAPHICAL USER INTERFACE

Matlab is a commercially available, widely used, interactive, technical computing software. Matlab versions 7.0 and higher provide serial communication functionality, GUI testing is a process to test application's user interface and to detect if application is functionally correct. GUI testing involves carrying set of tasks and comparing the result of same with the expected output and ability to repeat the same set of tasks multiple times with different data input and same level of accuracy. GUI testing can be performed both manually, by a human tester or could be performed automatically with the use of a software program. For this research, the GUI is used to show the authorized subject's name which is shown Figure 4.28 to 4.32.

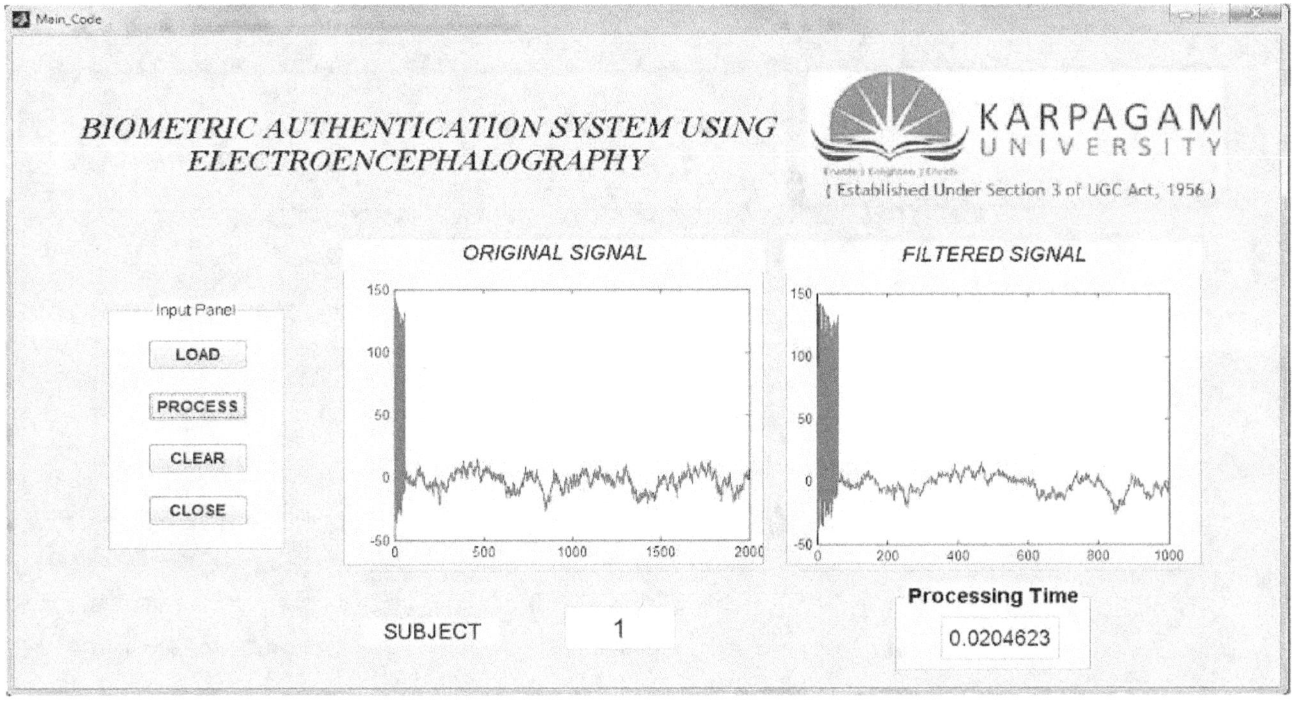

Figure 4.28 Analysis of EEG Signals Using GUI for Subject 1

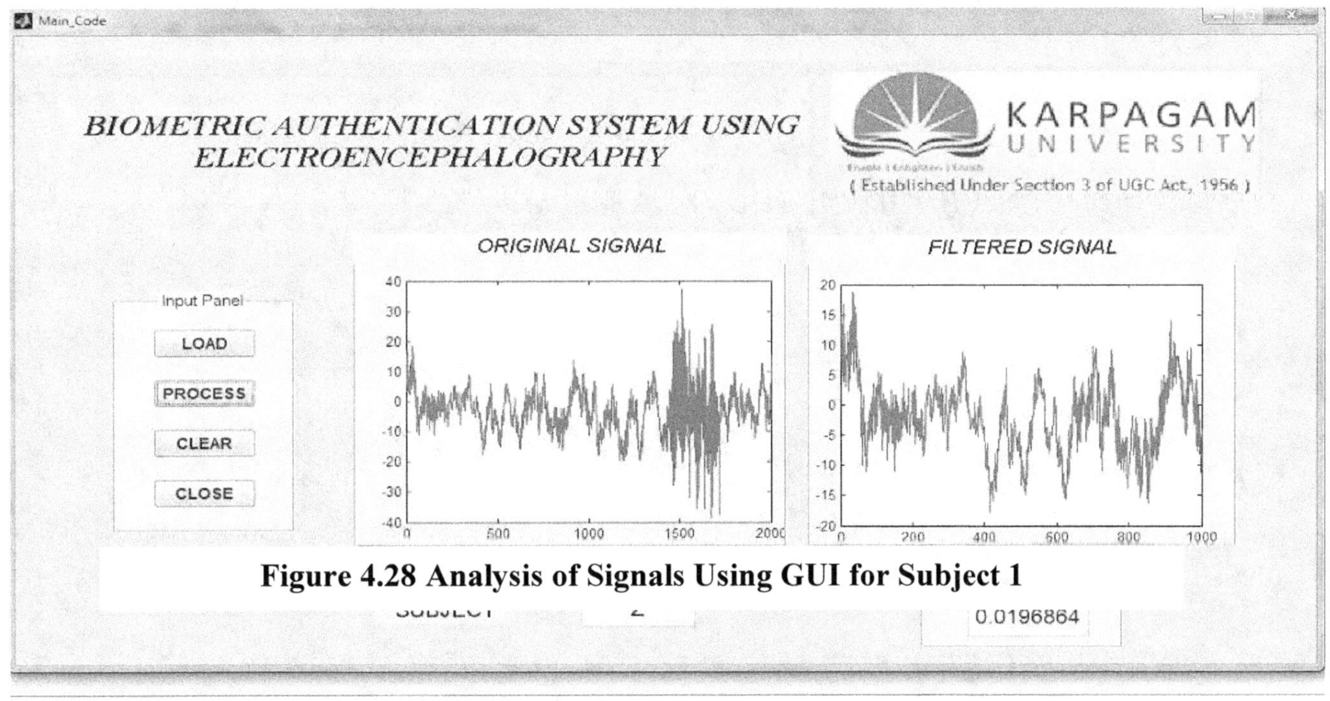

Figure 4.28 Analysis of Signals Using GUI for Subject 1

Figure 4.30 Analysis of EEG Signals Using GUI for Subject 2

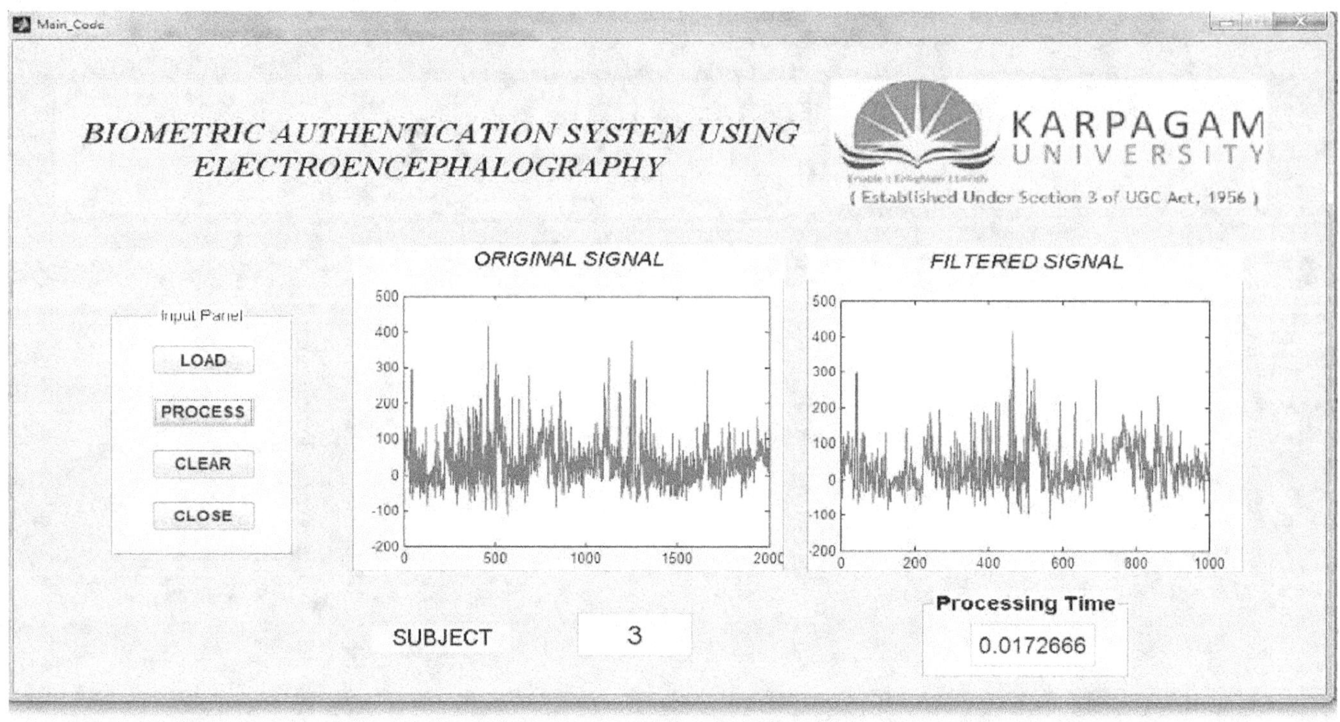

Figure 4.30 Analysis of EEG Signals Using GUI for Subject 3

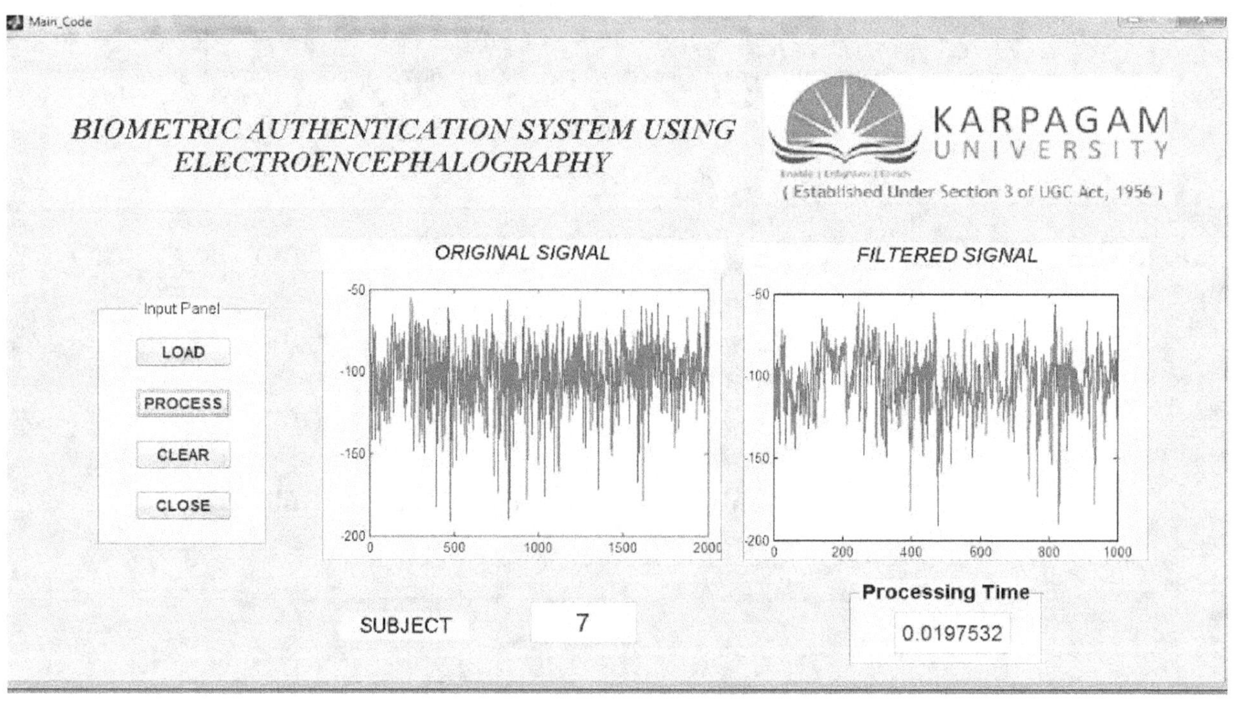

Figure 4.31 Analysis of EEG Signals Using GUI for Subject 7

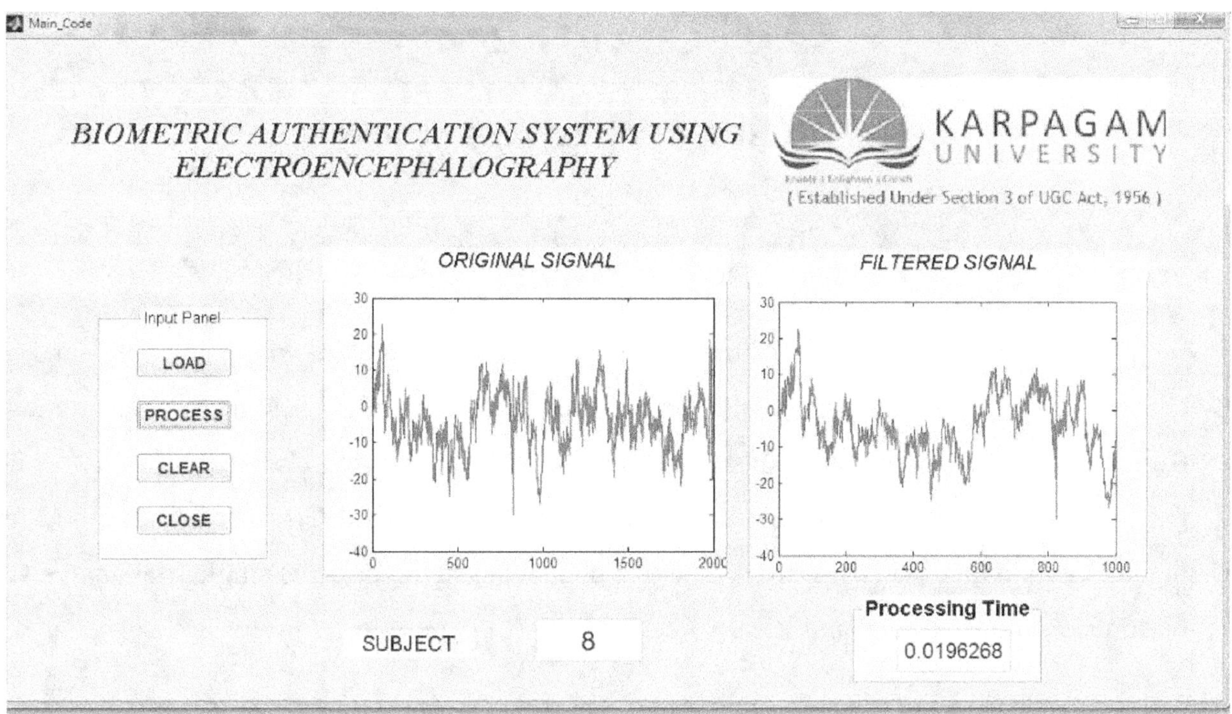

Figure 4.32 Analysis of EEG Signals Using GUI for Subject 8

4.10 SUMMARY

This chapter describes the feature extraction techniques and the classification process used. Feature extraction techniques, namely PSD with parametric and non parametric and high resolution methods are discussed briefly. Parametric methods, the Burg method, Covariance method, Modified Covariance and Yule- Walker methods are used. The techniques behind these methods are discussed briefly. In the non-parametric methods, Welch method is used and Multiple Signal Classification method from high resolution method is also used. In the classification process, two networks, namely FFNN and RNN are used for the classification of EEG brain signals. The different features of the network model, namely training time and testing time, no of input units, no of output units and no of hidden layers are discussed. A GUI system is developed for the final stage, which is verified the subjects for their corresponding signal. The performance result of these networks are discussed and tabulated in Appendix D to AA.

CHAPTER 5

RESULT AND DISCUSSION

5.1 INTRODUCTION

This chapter discusses about the classification results of single channel and two channels using FFFN and RNN with six feature extraction techniques, in parametric method Burg, Covariance, Modified Covariance and Yule-Walker methods are used. In the non-parametric methods Welch method is used and Multiple Signal Classification method from high resolution method is also used. The two channel system performs single trial analysis and bit transfer rate for FFNN and RNN.

5.2 SINGLE CHANNEL RESULTS OF FFNN AND RNN USING COVARIANCE ALGORITHM

Feature: PSD using Covariance

Training Network: Feed Forward Neural Network and Recurrent Neural Network

Training Algorithm: Back Propagation Training

The classification performance of the FFNN and RNN network model are find using Covariance algorithm features for the four tasks are shown in Table 5.1. Third and fourth column describes the percentage of training and testing data used in the experiments. Column five to eight shows the average value of maximum, minimum, mean and standard deviation of the classification performance of the networks for each task. The best classification performance are shown in Appendix D and E.

Table 5.1 Classification Results for FFNN and RNN Using Covariance Algorithm

Classifiers	Tasks	Training Time	Testing Time	PSD Using Covariance Algorithm			
				Max	Min	Mean	SD
Recognition Accuracy of FFNN	Read	2.55	0.45	94	90	92	1.31
	Relax	2.94	0.43	89	80	85	2.36
	Spell	5.64	0.45	89	85	87.45	1.39
	Maths	1.28	0.47	95	86	90.7	2.43
Recognition Accuracy of RNN	Read	5.14	0.94	83	79	81.3	3.77
	Relax	1.96	0.47	88	85	86.4	3.56
	Spell	2.43	0.43	92	88	90	3.25
	Maths	1.59	0.47	93	89	91.15	0.21

Figure 5.1 Performance analysis of FFNN and RNN Using Covariance Algorithm

The results for the Covariance feature using FFNN and RNN respectively, are shown in Table 5.1. Out of the 500 samples, 75% of the data were used to train the network and 100% of the data were used to test the network. The FFNN model was designed using 12 input neurons, 9 hidden neurons and 5 output neurons to verify the individuals. The hidden neurons were opted based on the trial and error method. The learning rate was chosen as 0.0001. Training was conducted until the average error had fallen below 0.001 or reached the maximum iteration limit of 1000 and testing error tolerance was fixed at 0.5. From the results, it was observed that the mean performance of the FFNN varied from 85% to 92% for   relax and read task. The standard deviation varied from 1.09 to 4.36. The training time ranged from

5.55 to 6.15 sec, while the testing time ranged from 0.72 Sec to 1.28 sec. The mean classification accuracy of RNN varied from 81.3% to 91.15%. Standard deviation varied from 0.21 to 3.77 for read and maths task. The training time varied from 7.96 sec to 16.06 sec, while the testing time ranged from 3.66 sec to 4.04 sec. The overall classification accuracy of 92% was obtained for Covariance algorithm using a FFNN network model for the read task are shown in Figure 5.1.

5.3 SINGLE CHANNEL RESULTS FOR FFNN AND RNN USING BURG ALGORITHM

Feature: PSD algorithm using Burg

Training network: Feed Forward Neural Network and Recurrent Neural Network

Training Algorithm: Back Propagation Training

The classification performance of the FFNN and RNN network model are find using Burg algorithm features for the four tasks is shown in Table 5.2. In the Table 5.2 third and fourth columns describe the percentage of training and testing data used in the experiments. Column five to eight shows the average values of maximum, minimum, mean and standard deviation of the classification performance of the networks for each task. The best performances are shown in Appendix F and G.

Table 5.2 Classification Results for FFNN and RNN Using Burg Algorithm

Classifiers	Tasks	Training Time	Testing Time	PSD Using Burg Algorithm			
				Max	Min	Mean	SD
Recognition Accuracy of FFNN	Read	1.66	0.46	90	85	87.6	3.23
	Relax	1.42	0.45	91	85	88.45	3.63
	Spell	1.2	0.43	84	80	83.9	2.6
	Maths	2.73	0.49	90	80	85.45	4.19
Recognition Accuracy of RNN	Read	7.66	0.47	92	89	90	4.61
	Relax	2.3	0.43	92	88	90	2.62
	Spell	1.72	0.02	98	92	95	2.59
	Maths	3.75	0.44	94	84	92	1.17

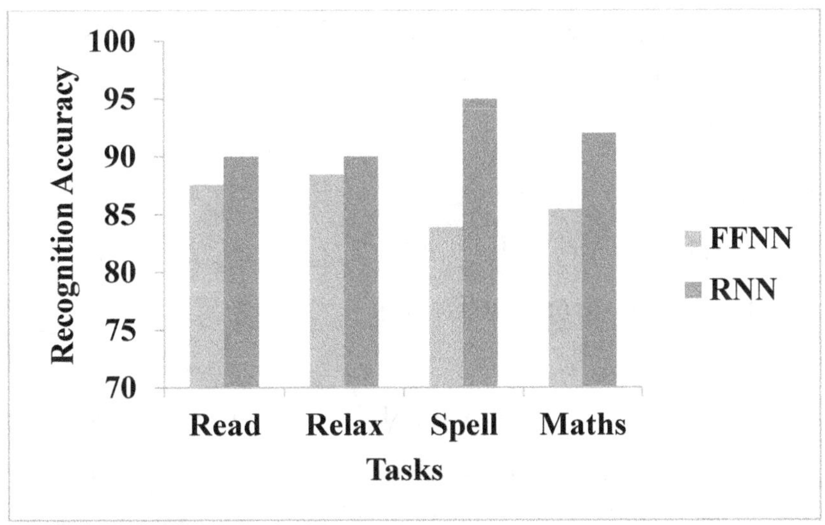

Figure 5.2 Performance Analysis of FFNN and RNN Using Burg Algorithm

The results for the Burg feature using FFNN and RNN respectively, are shown in Table 5.2. Out of the 500 samples, 75% of the data were used to train the network and 100% of the data were used to test the network. The FFNN model was designed using 12 input neurons, 9 hidden neurons and 5 output neurons to verify the individuals. The hidden neurons were opted based on the trial and error method. The learning rate was chosen as 0.0001. Training was conducted until the average error had fallen below 0.001 or reached the maximum iteration limit of 1000 and testing error tolerance was fixed at 0.5. From the results, it was observed that the mean performance of the FFNN varied from 83.9% to 88.45% for spell and relax task. The standard deviation varied from 2.6 to 4.19. The training time ranged from 1.2 Sec to 2.73 sec, while the testing time ranged from 0.43 sec to 0.49 sec. The mean classification accuracy of RNN varied from 90% to 95% read, relax and spell task. Standard deviation varied from 1.17 to 4.61. The training time varied from 1.72 sec to 7.66 sec, while the testing time ranged from 0.02 sec to 0.47 sec. The overall classification accuracy of 95% was obtained for covariance algorithm using RNN network model for the spell task is shown in Figure 5.2.

5.4 SINGLE CHANNEL RESULTS FOR FFNN AND RNN USING MODIFIED COVARIANCE ALGORITHM

Feature : PSD using Modified Covariance

Training network: Feed Forward Neural Network and Recurrent Neural Network

Training Algorithm: Back Propagation Training

The classification performance of the FFNN and RNN network model are find using Modified Covariance algorithm features for the four tasks is shown in Table 5.3. Third and fourth column describes the percentage of training and testing data used in the experiments. Five to eight shows the average values of maximum, minimum, mean and standard deviation of the classification performance of the networks for each task. The best performances are shown in Appendix H and I.

Table 5.3 Classification Results for FFNN and RNN Using Modified Covariance Algorithm

Classifiers	Tasks	Training Time	Testing Time	PSD Using Modified Covariance Algorithm			
				Max	Min	Mean	SD
Recognition Accuracy of FFNN	Read	5.91	1.17	90	81	85.2	3.39
	Relax	6.18	1.18	83	80	83.3	3.77
	Spell	5.9	1.09	90	80	85.45	3.97
	Maths	6.02	1.19	92	83	87.15	3.79
Recognition Accuracy of RNN	Read	6.83	1.12	92	82	87.8	3.88
	Relax	6.01	1.1	90	88	89	2.44
	Spell	6.44	1.21	95	89	92	3.67
	Maths	6.46	1.25	91	87	89.9	2.45

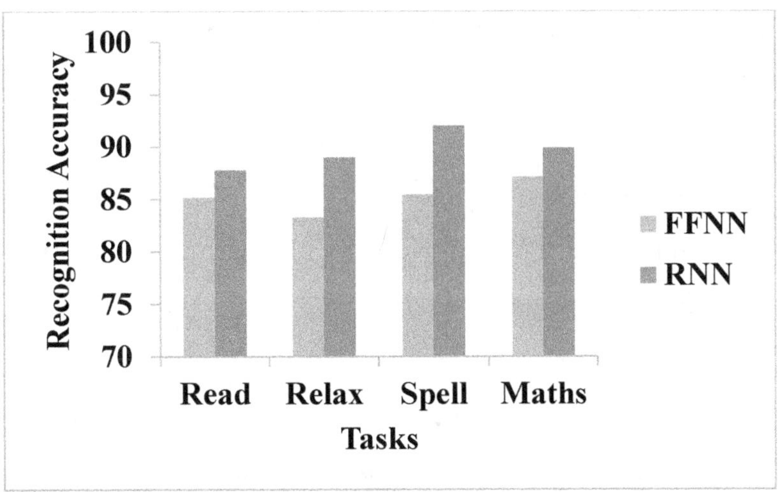

Figure 5.3 Performance Analysis of FFNN and RNN Using Modified Covariance Algorithm

The results for the Modified Covariance feature using FFNN and RNN respectively, is shown in Table 5.3. Out of the 500 samples, 75% of the data were used to train the network and 100% of the data were used to test the network. The FFNN model was designed using 12 input neurons, 9 hidden neurons and 5 output neurons to veify the individuals. The hidden neurons were opted based on the trial and error method. The learning rates were chosen as 0.0001. Training was conducted until the average error had fallen below 0.001 or reached the maximum iteration limit of 1000 and testing error tolerance was fixed at 0.5. From the results, it was observed that the mean performance of the FFNN varied from 83.3% to 87.15% for relax and maths. The standard deviation varied from 3.39 to 3.97. The training time ranged from 5.9 sec to 6.1 sec, while the testing time ranged from 1.09 sec to 1.19 sec. The mean classification accuracy of RNN varied from 87.8% to 92% for read and spell task. Standard deviation varied from 2.44 to 3.88 for relax and read task. The training time varied from 6.01 sec to 6.83 sec, while the testing time ranged from 1.1 sec to 1.25 sec. The overall classification accuracy of 92% was obtained for Modified Covariance algorithm using RNN network model for the spell task is shown in Figure 5.3.

5.5 SINGLE CHANNEL RESULTS OF FFNN AND RNN USING YULE-WALKER ALGORITHM

Feature: PSD using Yule-Walker algorithm

Training Network: Feed Forward Neural Network and Recurrent Neural Network

Training Algorithm: Back Propagation Training

The network performance is recorded for twenty trials and the average values are shown in Table 5.4 for the four biometric tasks, namely read, relax, spell and maths tasks. Third and fourth column describes the percentage of training and testing data used in the experiments. Column five to eight shows the average values of maximum, minimum, mean and standard deviation of the classification performance of the networks for each task. The best performances are shown in Appendix J and K.

Table 5.4 Classification Results for FFNN and RNN using Yule-Walker Algorithm

Classifiers	Tasks	Training Time	Testing Time	PSD Using Yule-Walker Algorithm			
				Max	Min	Mean	SD
Recognition Accuracy of FFNN	Read	5.49	0.55	90	83	86.28	2.19
	Relax	5.74	0.62	85	79	82	3.63
	Spell	5.78	0.53	90	83	87.65	3.92
	Maths	5.49	0.54	86	80	83	3.84
Recognition Accuracy of RNN	Read	5.68	0.54	88	87	87	2.56
	Relax	6.22	4.08	92	86	89	2.98
	Spell	6.05	0.54	92	87	92	3.25
	Maths	10.9	0.55	90	88	89	2.98

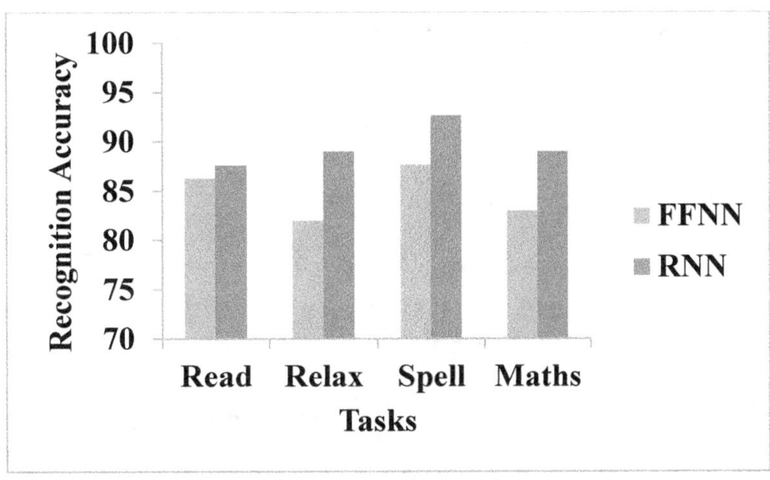

Figure 5.4 Performance Analysis of FFNN and RNN Using Yule- Walker Algorithm

The results for the Yule Walker feature using FFNN and RNN respectively, are shown in Table 5.4. Out of the 500 samples, 75% of the data were used to train the network and 100% of the data were used to test the network. The FFNN model was designed using 12 input neurons, 9 hidden neurons and 5 output neurons to verify the individuals. The hidden neurons were opted based on the trial and error method. The learning rate was chosen as 0.0001. Training was conducted until the average error had fallen below 0.001 or reached the maximum iteration limit of 1000 and testing error tolerance was fixed at 0.5. From the results, it was observed that the mean performance of the FFNN varied from 82% and 87.65% for relax and spell task. The standard deviation varied from 2.19 to 3.92. The training time ranged from 5.49 sec to 5.78 sec, while the testing time ranged from 0.53 sec to 0.62 sec. The mean classification accuracy of RNN varied from 87% to 92% for read and spell task. Standard deviation varied from 2.56 to 3.25. The training time varied from 5.68 sec to 10.9 sec, while the testing time ranged from 0.54 sec to 4.08 sec. The overall classification accuracy of 92% was obtained for Yule-Walker algorithm using RNN network model for the spell task are shown in Figure 5.4.

5.6 SINGLE CHANNEL RESULTS FOR FFNN AND RNN USING WELCH ALGORITHM

Feature: PSD algorithm using Welch Algorithm

Training Network: Feed Forward Neural Network and Recurrent Neural Network

Training Algorithm: Back Propagation Training

The network performance is recorded for twenty trials and the average values are shown in Table 5.5 for the four biometric tasks, namely read, relax, spell and maths tasks. Third and fourth column describes the percentage of training and testing data used in the experiments. Column five to eight shows the average values of maximum, minimum, mean and standard deviation of the classification performance of the networks for each task. The best performances are shown in Appendix L and M.

Table 5.5 Classification Results for FFNN and RNN using Welch Algorithm

Classifiers	Tasks	Training Time	Testing Time	PSD Using Welch Algorithm			
				Max	Min	Mean	SD
Recognition Accuracy of FFNN	Read	5.7	0.76	89	83	86.9	3.58
	Relax	5.72	0.69	87	78	82.8	2.34
	Spell	5.76	0.75	92	83	87.6	2.96
	Maths	5.57	0.68	89	85	87.5	3.35
Recognition Accuracy of RNN	Read	5.72	0.69	92	86	89	2.41
	Relax	5.75	0.72	95	83	89.9	1.28
	Spell	6.21	0.73	91	83	91.2	3.75
	Maths	6.11	0.70	90	88	89.6	2.61

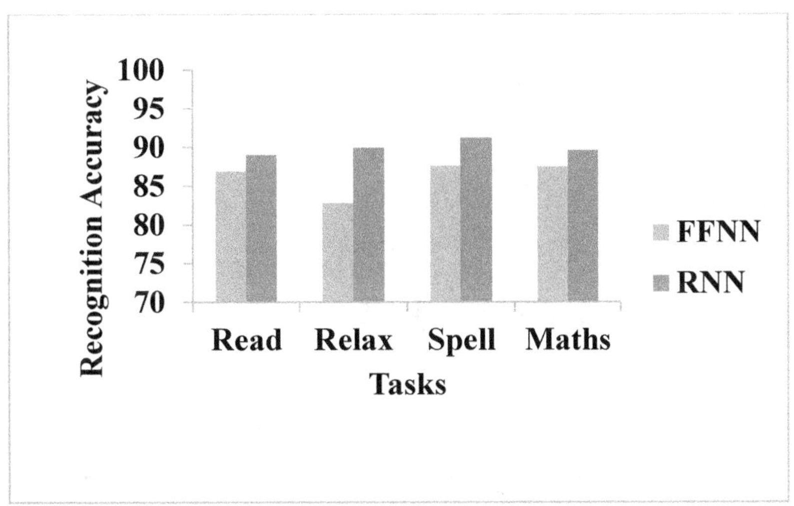

Figure 5.5 Performance Analysis of FFNN and RNN Using Welch Algorithm

The results for the Welch feature using FFNN and RNN respectively, are shown in Table 5.5. Out of the 500 samples, 75% of the data were used to train the network and 100% of the data were used to test the network. The FFNN model was designed using 12 input neurons, 9 hidden neurons and 5 output neurons to verify the individuals. The hidden neurons were opted based on the trial and error method. The learning rate was chosen as 0.0001. Training was conducted until the average error had fallen below 0.001 or reached the maximum iteration limit of 1000 and testing error tolerance was fixed at 0.5. From the results, it was observed that the mean performance of the FFNN varied from 82.8% to 87.6% for relax and spell task. The standard deviation varied from 2.34 to 3.58. The training time ranged from 5.57 sec to 5.76 sec, while the testing time ranged from 0.68 sec to 0.76 sec. The mean classification accuracy of RNN varied from 89% to 91.2% to for read and spell task. Standard deviation varied from 1.28 to 3.75. The training time varied from 5.72 to 6.21, while the testing time ranged from 0.69 sec to 0.73 sec. The overall classification accuracy of 91.2% was obtained for Welch algorithm using RNN network model for the spell task is shown in Figure 5.5.

5.7 SINGLE CHANNEL RESULTS FOR FFNN AND RNN USING MUSIC ALGORITHM

Feature: PSD algorithm using MUSIC Algorithm

Training Network: Feed Forward Neural Network and Recurrent Neural Network

Training Algorithm: Back Propagation Training

The network performance is recorded for twenty trials and the average values are shown in Table 5.6 for the four biometric tasks, namely read, relax, spell and maths tasks. Third and fourth column describes the percentage of training and testing data used in the experiments. Columns five to eight shows the average values of maximum, minimum, mean and standard deviation of the classification performance of the networks for each task. The average and maximum classification was taken. The best performances are shown in Appendix N and O.

Table 5.6 Classification Results for FFNN and RNN Using MUSIC Algorithms

Classifiers	Tasks	Training Time	Testing Time	PSD Using Multiple Signal Classification Algorithm			
				Max	Min	Mean	SD
Recognition Accuracy of FFNN	Read	5.91	0.54	92	83	87.8	3.25
	Relax	6.05	0.54	90	83	86.55	3.38
	Spell	6.02	0.24	90	82	86	3.52
	Maths	6.11	0.54	85	78	81.9	1.56
Recognition Accuracy of RNN	Read	6.06	0.58	95	83	89.8	3.35
	Relax	6.24	0.56	93	85	89	3.23
	Spell	5.67	0.59	91	89	90.65	1.65
	Maths	5.67	0.59	92	88	90	1.38

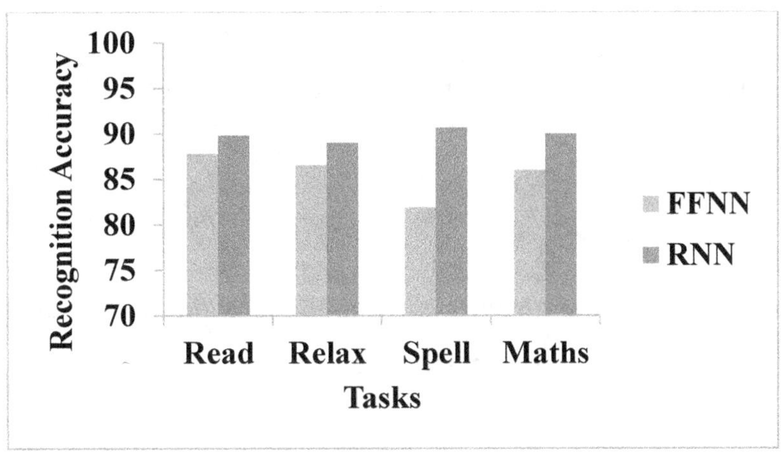

Figure 5.6 Performance Analysis of FFNN and RNN Using MUSIC Algorithms

The results for the MUSIC feature using FFNN and RNN respectively, are shown in Table 5.6. Out of the 500 samples, 75% of the data were used to train the network and 100% of the data were used to test the network. The FFNN model was designed using 12 input neurons, 9 hidden neurons and 5 output neurons to verify the individuals. The hidden neurons were opted based on the trial and error method. The learning rate was chosen as 0.0001. Training was conducted until the average error had fallen below 0.001 or reached maximum iteration limit of 1000 and testing error tolerance was fixed at 0.5. From the results, it was observed that the mean performance of the FFNN varied from 81.9% to 87.8% for spell and read task. The standard deviation varied from 1.56 to 3.38. The training time ranged from 5.91sec to 6.11sec, while the testing time ranged from 0.24 sec to 0.54 sec. The mean classification accuracy of RNN varied from 89% to 90.65% for relax and spell task. Standard deviation varied from 1.38 to 3.35. The training time varied from 5.67sec to 6.24 sec, while the testing time ranged from 0.56 sec to 0.59 sec. The overall classification accuracy of 90.65% was obtained for MUSIC algorithm using RNN network model for the spell task are shown in Figure 5.6.

METHOD: 2

5.8 TWO CHANNEL RESULTS OF FFNN AND RNN USING COVARIANCE ALGORITHM

Feature: PSD using Covariance Algorithm

Training Network: Feed Forward Neural Network and Recurrent Neural Network

Training Algorithm: Back Propagation Training

The network performance is recorded for twenty trials and the average values are shown in Table 5.7 for the four biometric tasks, namely read, relax, spell and maths tasks. Third and fourth column describes the percentage of training and testing data used in the experiments. Column five to eight shows the average values of maximum, minimum, mean and standard deviation of the classification performance of the networks for each task. The best performances are shown in Appendix P and Q.

Table 5.7 Classification Results for FFNN and RNN Using Covariance Algorithm

Classifiers	Tasks	Training Time	Testing Time	PSD Using Covariance Algorithm			
				Max	Min	Mean	SD
Recognition Accuracy of FFNN	Read	5.17	3.64	99	80	92.5	4.36
	Relax	11.4	3.79	95	80	87.8	3.4
	Spell	2.93	6.82	100	95	97	1.86
	Maths	0.6	5.61	99	96	97.85	1.09
Recognition Accuracy of RNN	Read	10.8	2.56	95	80	87.35	4.75
	Relax	5.71	0.52	96	88	91.9	2.22
	Spell	5.55	1.07	99	90	97	2.13
	Maths	5.55	1.07	99	90	95.25	3.14

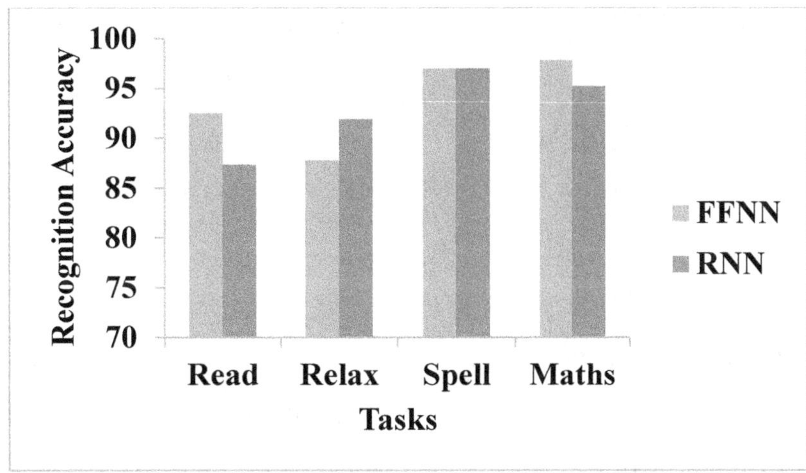

Figure 5.7 Performance Analysis of FFNN and RNN Using Covariance Algorithm

The results for the Covariance feature using FFNN and RNN respectively, are shown in Table 5.7. Out of the 500 samples, 75% of the data were used to train the network and 100% of the data were used to test the network. The FFNN model was designed using 24 input neurons, 9 hidden neurons and 4 output neurons to verify the individuals. The hidden neurons were opted based on the trial and error method. The learning rate was chosen as 0.0001. Training was conducted until the average error had fallen below 0.001 or reached maximum iteration limit of 1000 and testing error tolerance was fixed at 0.5. From the results, it was observed that the mean performance of the FFNN varied from 87.8% to 97.85% for relax and maths task. The standard deviation varied from 1.09 to 4.36. The training time ranged from 0.6 sec to 5.17 sec, while the testing time ranged from 3.64 sec to 6.82 sec. The mean classification accuracy of RNN varied from 87.35% to 97% for read and spell task. Standard deviation varied from 2.13 to 4.75. The training time varied from 5.55 sec to 10.8 sec, while the testing time ranged from 0.52 sec to 2.56 sec. The overall classification accuracy of 97.85% was obtained for Covariance algorithm using FFNN network model for the maths task is shown in Figure 5.7.

5.9 TWO CHANNEL RESULTS FOR FFNN AND RNN USING BURG ALGORITHM

Feature: PSD using Burg Algorithm

Training Network: Feed Forward Neural Network and Recurrent Neural Network

Training Algorithm: Back Propagation Training

The network performance is recorded for twenty trials and the average values are shown in Table 5.8 for the four biometric tasks, namely read, relax, spell and maths tasks. Third and fourth column describes the percentage of training and testing data used in the experiments. Column five to eight shows the average values of maximum, minimum, mean and standard deviation of the classification performance of the networks for each task. The best performances are shown in Appendix R and S.

Table 5.8 Classification Results for FFNN and RNN using Burg Algorithm

Classifiers	Tasks	Training Time	Testing Time	PSD Using Burg Algorithm			
				Max	Min	Mean	SD
Recognition Accuracy of FFNN	Read	5.87	0.57	96	89	92.1	2.05
	Relax	5.77	9.58	93	80	87.15	3.34
	Maths	2.95	0.44	97	82	87.15	5.24
	Spell	5.97	0.55	98	95	92.15	3.59
Recognition Accuracy of RNN	Read	5.55	1.07	99	95	97.9	1.29
	Relax	5.87	0.57	94	89	91	1.38
	Maths	5.64	1.08	99	94	97	1.39
	Spell	5.61	0.6	99	96	98.05	0.76

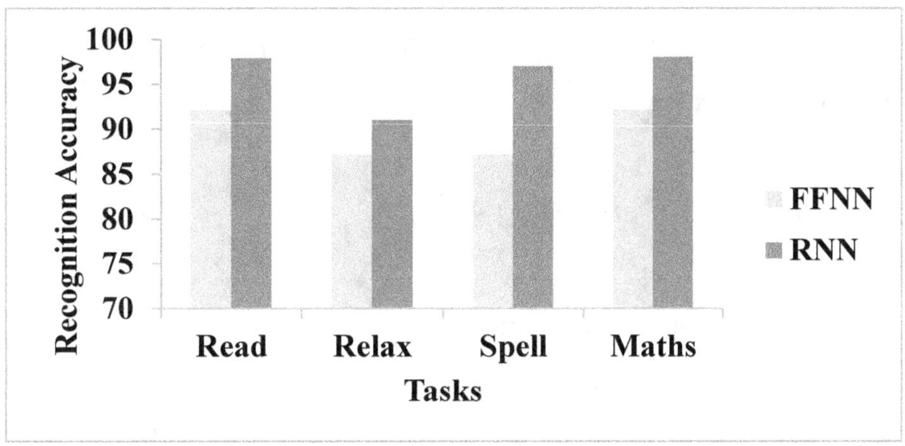

Figure 5.8 Classifications Performance of FFNN and RNN Using Burg Algorithm

The results for the Burg feature using FFNN and RNN respectively, are shown in Table 5.8. Out of the 500 samples, 75% of the data were used to train the network and 100% of the data were used to test the network. The FFNN model was designed using 24 input neurons, 9 hidden neurons and 4 output neurons to verify the individuals. The hidden neurons were opted based on the trial and error method. The learning rate was chosen as 0.0001. Training was conducted until the average error had fallen below 0.001 or reached the maximum iteration limit of 1000 and testing error tolerance was fixed at 0.5. From the results, it was observed that the mean performance of the FFNN varied from 87.15% to 92.15% for relax, maths and spell task. The standard deviation varied from 2.05 to 5.24. The training time ranged from 2.95 to 5.97 sec, while the testing time ranged from 0.55 sec to 9.58 sec. The mean classification accuracy of RNN varied from 91% to 98.05% for relax and spell task. Standard deviation varied from 0.76 to 1.39 for spell and maths task. The training time varied from 5.55 sec to 5.87 sec, while the testing time ranged from 0.6 sec to 1.08 sec. The overall classification accuracy of 98.05% was obtained for Burg algorithm using RNN network model for the spell task is shown in Figure 5.8.

5.10 TWO CHANNEL RESULTS FOR FFNN AND RNN USING MODIFIED COVARIANCE ALGORITHM

Feature: PSD using Modified Covariance Algorithm

Training Network: Feed Forward Neural Network and Recurrent Neural Network

Training Algorithm: Back Propagation Training

The network performance is recorded for twenty trials and the average values are shown in Table 5.9 for the four biometric tasks, namely read, relax, spell and maths tasks. Third and fourth column describes the percentage of training and testing data used in the experiments. Column five to eight shows the average values of maximum, minimum, mean and standard deviation of the classification performance of the networks for each task. The best performance shown in Appendix T, U.

Table 5.9 Classification Results for FFNN and RNN Using Modified Covariance Algorithm

Classifiers	Tasks	Training Time	Testing Time	Psd Using Modified Covariance Algorithm			
				Max	Min	Mean	SD
Recognition Accuracy of FFNN	Read	22.62	3.09	87	78	82.8	2.34
	Relax	19.93	2.07	95	82	88.5	3.75
	Maths	5.95	0.71	93	83	90.85	1.31
	Spell	5.77	9.58	94	87	90.9	1.74
Recognition Accuracy of RNN	Read	5.85	0.56	99	96	97.5	0.95
	Relax	5.77	9.58	95	89	91.75	1.45
	Maths	6.07	0.54	98	90	95.15	2.01
	Spell	5.78	1.13	99	94	97.55	1.28

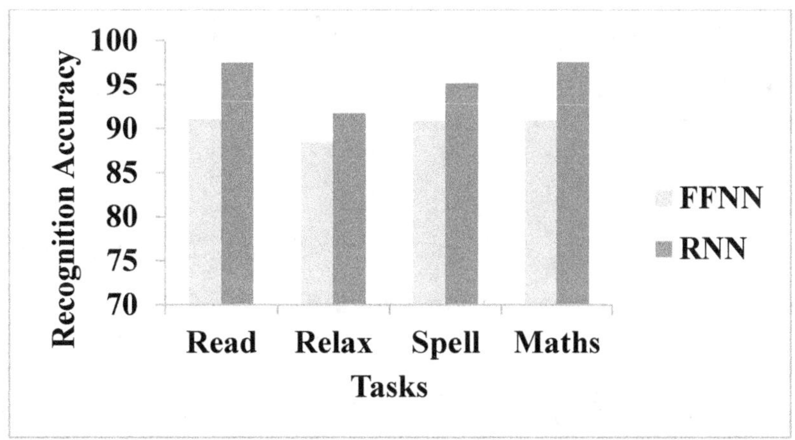

Figure 5.9 Performance Analysis of FFNN and RNN Using Modified Covariance Algorithm

The results for the Modified Covariance feature using FFNN and RNN respectively, are shown in Table 5.9. Out of the 500 samples, 75% of the data were used to train the network and 100% of the data were used to test the network. The FFNN model was designed using 24 input neurons, 9 hidden neurons and 4 output neurons to verify the individuals. The hidden neurons were opted based on the trial and error method. The learning rate was chosen as 0.0001. Training was conducted until the average error had fallen below 0.001 or reached the maximum iteration limit of 1000 and testing error tolerance was fixed at 0.5. From the results, it was observed that the mean performance of the FFNN varied from 88.5% to 91.05% for relax and read task. The standard deviation varied from 1.31 to 4.11. The training time ranged from 5.77 to 22.62 sec, while the testing time ranged from 0.71 sec to 9.58 sec. The mean classification accuracy of RNN varied from 91.75 % to 97.55% for relax and spell task. Standard deviation varied from 0.95 to 2.01. The training time varied from 5.77 sec to 6.07 sec, while the testing time ranged from 0.54 sec to 9.58 sec. The overall classification accuracy of 97.55% was obtained for Modified Covariance algorithm using RNN network model for the spell task are shown in Figure 5.9. The best performances is shown in appendix S and T.

5.11 TWO CHANNEL RESULTS FOR FFNN AND RNN USING YULE WALKER ALGORITHM

Feature: PSD using Yule Walker Algorithm

Training Network: Feed Forward Neural Network and Recurrent Neural Network

Training Algorithm: Back Propagation Training

The network performance is recorded for twenty trials and the average values are shown in Table 5.10 for the four biometric tasks namely read, relax, spell and maths tasks. Third and fourth column describes the percentage of training and testing data used in the experiments. Column five to eight shows the average values of maximum, minimum, mean and standard deviation of the classification performance of the networks for each task. The best performances are shown in Appendix V and W.

Table 5.10 Classification Results for FFNN and RNN Using Yule- Walker Algorithm

Classifiers	Tasks	Training Time	Testing Time	PSD Using Yule- Walker Algorithm			
				Max	Min	Mean	SD
Recognition Accuracy of FFNN	Read	6.03	1.01	98	80	94.7	4.13
	Relax	2.95	0.44	97	81	86	5.24
	Maths	5.55	1.07	99	90	95.9	2.31
	Spell	5.67	1.06	98	90	96.75	2.00
Recognition Accuracy of RNN	Read	6.03	1.01	98	95	96.7	1.17
	Relax	6.07	0.59	95	89	91.7	1.72
	Maths	6.1	0.58	99	91	96.55	1.57
	Spell	6.34	0.56	98	95	96.6	0.99

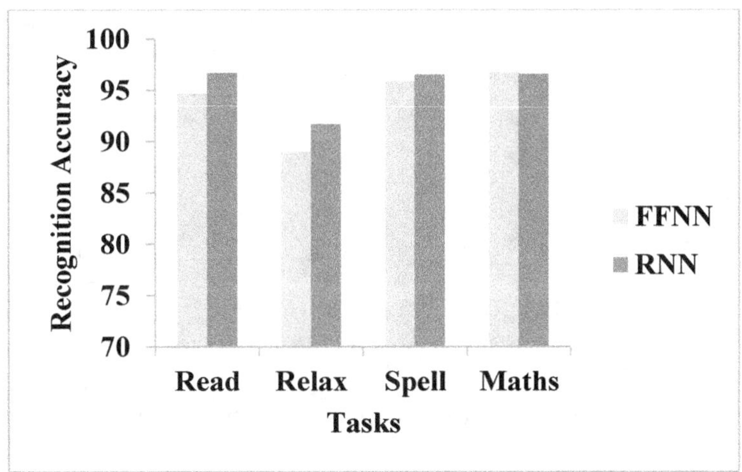

Figure 5.10 Performance Analysis of FFNN and RNN Using Yule -Walker Algorithm

The results for the Yule-Walker feature using FFNN and RNN respectively, are shown in Table 5.10. Out of the 500 samples, 75% of the data were used to train the network and 100% of the data were used to test the network. The FFNN model was designed using 24 input neurons, 9 hidden neurons and 4 output neurons to verify the individuals. The hidden neurons were opted based on the trial and error method. The learning rate was chosen as 0.0001. Training was conducted until the average error had fallen below 0.001 or reached the maximum iteration limit of 1000 and testing error tolerance was fixed at 0.5. From the results, it was observed that the mean performance of the FFNN varied from 89% to 96.75% for relax and spell task. The standard deviation varied from 2 to 4.44. The training time ranged from 5.55 sec to 8.92 sec, while the testing time ranged from 1.01 sec to 1.43 sec. The mean classification accuracy of RNN varied from 91.7% to 96.6% for relax and spell task. Standard deviation performance ranged from 0.99 to 1.72.The training time varied from 6.03 sec to 6.34 sec, while the testing time ranged from 0.56 sec to 1.01 sec. The overall classification accuracy of 96.75% was obtained for Yule-Walker algorithm using FFNN network model for the spell task is shown in Figure 5.10.

5.12 TWO CHANNEL RESULTS FOR FFNN AND RNN USING WELCH ALGORITHM

Feature: PSD using Welch Algorithm

Training Network: Feed Forward Neural Network and Recurrent Neural Network

Training Algorithm: Back Propagation Training

The network performance is recorded for twenty trials and the average values are shown in Table 5.11 for the four biometric tasks namely read, relax, spell and maths tasks. Third and fourth column describes the percentage of training and testing data used in the experiments. Column five to eight shows the average values of maximum, minimum, mean and standard deviation of the classification performance of the networks for each task. The best performances are shown in Appendix X and Y.

Table 5.11 Classification Results for FFNN and RNN Using Welch Algorithm

Classifiers	Tasks	Training Time	Testing Time	PSD Using Welch Algorithm			
				Max	Min	Mean	SD
Recognition Accuracy of FFNN	Read	6.24	0.56	96	88	91.35	2.15
	Relax	6.02	5.24	95	87	91.4	1.93
	Maths	5.88	0.69	99	85	91.05	3.62
	Spell	6.02	5.24	95	89	91.7	3.45
Recognition Accuracy of RNN	Read	5.78	1.13	99	97	96	0.56
	Relax	5.97	0.55	96	88	91.7	2.36
	Maths	5.64	1.08	99	97.5	95	1.36
	Spell	5.55	1.07	99	95	97	1.38

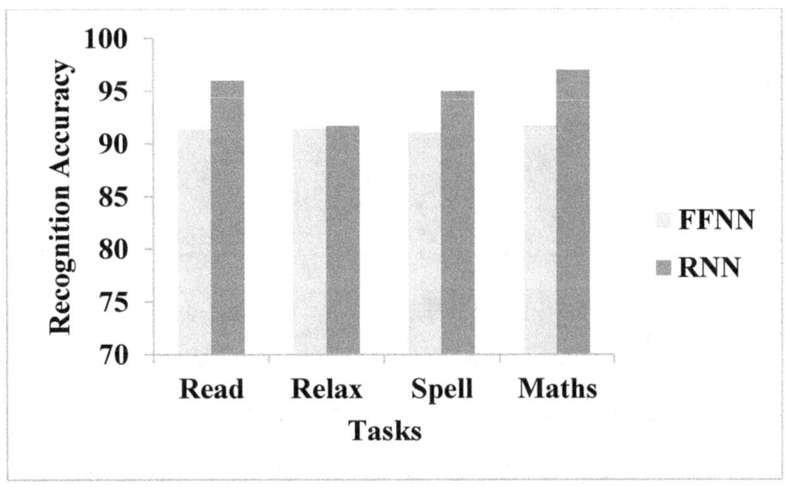

Figure 5.11 Performance Analysis of FFNN and RNN Using Welch Algorithm

The results for the Welch feature using FFNN and RNN respectively, are shown in Table 5.11. Out of the 500 samples, 75% of the data were used to train the network and 100% of the data were used to test the network. The FFNN model was designed using 24 input neurons, 9 hidden neurons and 4 output neurons to verify the individuals. The hidden neurons were opted based on the trial and error method. The learning rate was chosen as 0.0001. Training was conducted until the average error had fallen below 0.001 or reached the maximum iteration limit of 1000 and testing error tolerance was fixed at 0.5. From the results, it was observed that the mean performance of the FFNN varied from 91.05% to 91.7% for maths and spell task. The standard deviation varied from 1.93 to 3.62. The training time ranged from 5.88 sec to 6.24 sec, while the testing time ranged from 0.56 sec to 5.24 sec. The mean classification accuracy of RNN varied from 91.7% to 97% for relax and spell task. Standard deviation varied from 0.56 to 2.36 for read and relax task. The training time varied from 5.55 sec to 5.97 sec, while the testing time ranged from 0.55 sec to 1.13 sec. The overall classification accuracy of 97% was obtained for Welch using RNN network model for the spell task is shown in Figure 5.11.

5.13 TWO CHANNEL RESULTS FOR FFNN AND RNN USING MUSIC ALGORITHM

Feature: PSD Multiple Signal Classification Algorithm

Training Network: Feed Forward Neural Network and Recurrent Neural Network

Training Algorithm: Back Propagation Training

The network performance is recorded for twenty trials and the average values are shown in Table 5.12 for the four biometric tasks, namely read, relax, spell and maths tasks. Third and fourth column describes the percentage of training and testing data used in the experiments. Column five to eight shows the average values of maximum, minimum, mean and standard deviation of the classification performance of the networks for each task. The best performances are shown in Appendix Z and AA.

Table 5.12 Classification Results for FFNN and RNN Using MUSIC Algorithms

Classifiers	Tasks	Training Time	Testing Time	PSD Using MUSIC Algorithm			
				Max	Min	Mean	SD
Recognition Accuracy of FFNN	Read	5.97	0.55	94	85	90.55	2.63
	Relax	5.77	9.58	92	80	88.85	3.12
	Maths	5.97	0.55	96	85	91	2.41
	Spell	5.77	9.58	95	88	91.75	1.83
Recognition Accuracy of RNN	Read	5.8	0.58	98	92	96.35	1.57
	Relax	5.87	0.57	94	89	91.4	1.54
	Maths	5.52	1.54	98	95	96.5	0.89
	Spell	5.69	1.05	98	95	97	1.03

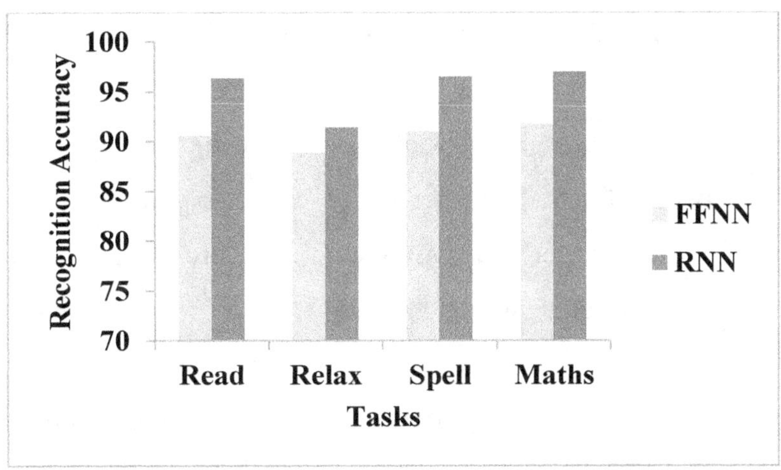

Figure 5.12 Classifications Performance of FFNN and RNN Using MUSIC Algorithms

The results for the MUSIC feature using FFNN and RNN respectively, are shown in Table 5.12. Out of the 500 samples, 75% of the data were used to train the network and 100% of the data were used to test the network. The FFNN model was designed using 24 input neurons, 9 hidden neurons and 4 output neurons to verify the individuals. The hidden neurons were opted based on the trial and error method. The learning rate was chosen as 0.0001. Training was conducted until the average error had fallen below 0.001 or reached the maximum iteration limit of 1000 and testing error tolerance was fixed at 0.5. From the results, it was observed that the mean performance of the FFNN varied from 88.85% to 91.75% for relax and spell task. The standard deviation varied from 1.83 to 3.12. The training time ranged from 5.7 sec to 5.97 sec, while the testing time ranged from 0.55 sec to 9.58 sec. The mean classification accuracy of RNN varied from 91.4% to 97% for relax and spell task. Standard deviation varied from 0.89 to 1.57. The training time varied from 5.52 sec to 5.87 sec, while the testing time ranged from 0.57 sec to 1.54 sec. The overall classification accuracy of 97% was obtained for music algorithm using RNN network model for the spell task are shown in Figure 5.12.

5.14 COMPARISON BETWEEN SINGLE CHANNEL AND TWO CHANNELS

Experiments are conducted to model networks using four biometric tasks and six PSD features and two networks for both single channel and two channel data. 48 network models, each are analyzed single channel and two channel data are both analyzed using 96 network models. The experimental analysis of the 96 network models shows the two channel acquisition methods give marginally better recognition rate compared to the single channel acquisition method. A maximum recognition rate of 98.05% was obtained by Burg algorithm using RNN method are shown in Figure 5.13.

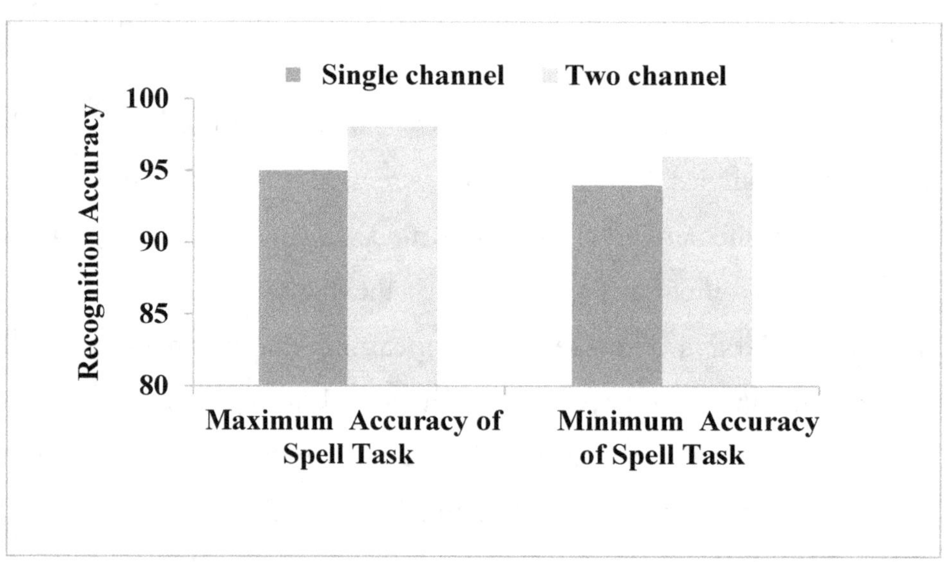

Figure 5.13 Performance Analysis of the RNN for Single Channel and Two Channel Process using the Burg Features

5.15 SINGLE TRIAL ANALYSIS

The analysis of single trial responses of field potentials is an important tool to study brain signals. Single trial analysis can indeed provide additional information that is obscured or simply not available in the average responses. The importance of studying single trial responses is reinforced by the fact that different brain processes are correlated with trial-by-trial variation of the responses. The two channel system is better than the single channel system. So in two channel system we prefer single trial analysis and predictive power analysis. The single trial EEG signals for the four biometric tasks are classified by PSD using FFNN and RNN. The result of the single trial classification for the individual subject shown in Table 5.13 below. Here single trail analysis is performed for FFNN and RNN networks using two channel systems.

5.16 SINGLE TRIAL ANALYSIS FOR FFNN

Table 5.13 Covariance Feature Using FFNN Model

SINGLE TRIAL ANALYSIS					
Tasks Subjects	Event			Non -Event	
	Read	Maths	Spell	Relax	Unknown
S1	6	7	9	7	11
S2	9	10	8	7	6
S3	6	8	8	7	11
S4	7	7	9	6	11
S5	6	8	9	8	11
S6	6	9	10	6	9
S7	7	6	7	9	9
S8	7	7	9	9	8
S9	6	7	9	9	9
S10	9	8	9	8	6
S11	6	9	6	7	12
S12	6	7	10	7	10
S13	9	9	10	8	6
S14	8	9	10	7	4
S15	6	7	9	9	6
S16	6	9	8	6	9
S17	9	8	10	8	11
S18	6	8	7	7	5
S19	6	6	9	8	12
S20	6	7	8	8	11
S21	8	7	8	8	9
S22	7	9	10	7	7
S23	6	8	7	6	13
S24	6	8	8	8	10
S25	7	7	8	8	10

The performance of four biometric tasks, designed for each subject was verified through a single trial analysis using a FFNN for Covariance features are shown in Table 5.13, it was observed that the acceptance rate of S2, S5, S9, S13, S15, S17, S19 and S22 was high at a mean of 85%. It is evident that 80% of the signal had a recognition rate of eight and above. For some subjects like S4, S7, S12, S18, and S24 the recognition rates were not appreciable. From the analysis we were able to conclude that more training data is required to improve the recognition accuracy of events. From the result it was observed that the feasibility of designing a biometric system is possible for some subject using covariance feature for FFNN, while for some of the subjects like S4, S7, S12, S18, and S24 the mean accuracy of four tasks biometric system was around 80%. Hence, more training was required.

Table 5.14 Burg Feature Using FFNN Model

SINGLE TRIAL ANALYSIS					
Tasks	Event			Non -Event	
	Read	Maths	Spell	Relax	Unknown
Subjects					
S1	8	7	8	6	11
S2	9	9	9	8	5
S3	7	8	8	7	10
S4	8	8	9	8	7
S5	9	8	9	9	5
S6	8	8	9	7	8
S7	7	8	9	7	9
S8	9	9	9	5	7
S9	9	7	9	6	9
S10	9	7	10	4	10
S11	9	8	9	3	13
S12	8	6	8	2	14
S13	9	10	10	8	3
S14	8	8	9	7	8
S15	9	7	9	8	7
S16	6	6	9	6	13
S17	9	7	8	6	10
S18	6	8	9	7	10
S19	6	6	8	8	12
S20	6	7	8	8	11
S21	6	7	9	6	12
S22	9	7	10	9	5
S23	8	9	9	7	7
S24	6	7	9	8	10
S25	6	7	8	8	11

The performance of the four biometric tasks designed for each subject was verified through a single trial analysis using a FFNN for PSD algorithm using Burg features are shown in Table 5.14. From the Table 5.14 it was observed the acceptance rate of S2, S4, S5, S9, S13, S15, S17 and S22 was high at a mean of 90%, it is evident that eighty percentage of the signal had a recognition rate of nine and above. For some subjects like S1, S7, S11, S12, S20 and S21 the recognition rates were not appreciable from the analysis, hence to conclude more training is required to improve the recognition accuracy of events. From the result, it was observed that the feasibility of designing a biometric system is possible for some subject using Burg feature for FFNN, while some of the subjects like S1, S7, S11, S12, S20 and S21 the mean accuracy of four task biometric systems was around 70% only. Hence, more training was required.

Table 5.15 Modified Covariance Feature Using FFNN Model

SINGLE TRIAL ANALYSIS					
Tasks	Event			Non -Event	
Subjects	Read	Maths	Spell	Relax	Unknown
S1	8	7	10	8	7
S2	8	10	10	6	6
S3	6	8	10	7	9
S4	9	7	9	8	7
S5	9	8	8	9	6
S6	8	9	10	7	6
S7	7	6	7	4	16
S8	7	7	9	6	11
S9	8	7	8	9	8
S10	7	8	8	10	7
S11	9	9	10	5	7
S12	6	7	10	5	12
S13	7	7	10	6	10
S14	8	7	10	4	11
S15	9	10	9	9	3
S16	7	6	8	6	13
S17	7	7	7	9	10
S18	7	8	7	7	11
S19	10	9	9	14	5
S20	6	6	8	10	10
S21	8	7	8	5	12
S22	7	7	10	8	8
S23	8	8	7	4	13
S24	6	9	8	6	11
S25	6	7	9	8	10

The performance of the four biometric tasks is designed for each subject and was verified through a single trial analysis using a FFNN for PSD algorithm using Modified Covariance features are shown in Table 5.15. From the Table 5.15 it was observed the acceptance rate S1, S2, S5, S9, S10, S11, S15, S19 and S22 was was high at a mean of 85%, it is evident that eighty percentage of the signal had a recognition rate of eight and above. For some subjects like S3, S7, S12, S14, S17 and S25 the recognition rates were not appreciable. From the analysis were able to conclude more training data is required to improve the recognition accuracy of events. From the result it was observed that the feasibility of designing a biometric system is possible for some subject using Modified Covariance feature for FFNN, while for some of the subjects like S3, S7, S12, S14, S17 and S25 the mean accuracy of four tasks biometric systems was around 70%. Hence, more training was required.

Table 5.16 Yule -Walker Feature Using FFNN Model

SINGLE TRIAL ANALYSIS					
Tasks / Subjects	Event			Non -Event	
	Read	Maths	Spell	Relax	Unknown
S1	10	8	9	7	6
S2	7	7	8	7	11
S3	8	7	8	7	10
S4	7	8	9	6	10
S5	8	7	9	8	10
S6	9	7	10	6	8
S7	6	6	7	9	12
S8	7	6	9	9	9
S9	8	5	9	9	9
S10	9	9	9	8	5
S11	8	7	6	7	12
S12	8	6	10	7	9
S13	9	7	10	8	6
S14	8	9	10	7	6
S15	9	7	9	9	6
S16	8	9	8	6	9
S17	8	8	10	8	6
S18	6	8	7	7	12
S19	7	6	9	8	10
S20	6	7	8	8	11
S21	8	7	8	8	9
S22	7	9	10	7	9
S23	6	8	7	6	13
S24	6	8	8	8	10
S25	7	7	8	8	10

The Performance of the four biometric tasks designed for each subject is verified through a Single trial analysis using a FFNN for PSD algorithm using Yule -Walker features are shown in Table 5.16. It was observed the acceptance rate S1, S5, S8, S9, S10, S13, S14, S15, S17 and S22 was high at a mean of 80%, it is evident that eighty percentage of the signal had a recognition rate of eight and above. For some subjects like S2, S4, S11, S19, S21, S23 and S24 the recognition rates were not appreciable from the analysis were able to conclude more training was required to improve the recognition accuracy of events. From the result it was observed that the feasibility of designing a biometric system is possible for some subject using Yule -Walker feature for FFNN, while for some of the subjects like S2, S4, S11, S19, S21, S23 and S24 the mean accuracy of four tasks biometric system was around 75%. Hence, more training was required.

Table 5.17 Welch Feature Using FFNN Model

SINGLE TRIAL ANALYSIS					
Tasks \ Subjects	Event			Non -Event	
	Read	Maths	Spell	Relax	Unknown
S1	9	7	9	7	8
S2	8	9	10	7	6
S3	7	8	9	7	9
S4	7	8	7	6	12
S5	6	8	9	8	9
S6	7	7	10	6	10
S7	8	9	7	9	7
S8	8	10	9	9	4
S9	8	9	9	9	5
S10	10	8	9	8	5
S11	7	7	6	7	13
S12	7	6	10	7	10
S13	9	9	10	8	4
S14	9	10	10	7	4
S15	8	8	10	9	5
S16	10	9	8	6	7
S17	9	8	10	8	5
S18	8	8	9	7	8
S19	8	6	9	8	9
S20	6	7	8	8	11
S21	8	7	8	8	9
S22	7	9	10	7	7
S23	6	8	6	6	14
S24	6	8	8	8	10
S25	7	9	8	8	8

The performance of the four biometric tasks designed for each subject and is verified through a single trial analysis using a FFNN for PSD algorithm using Welch features are shown in Table 5.17. It was observed the acceptance rate for S2, S5, S7, S8, S9, S10, S13, S17, and S22 was high at a mean of 85%. It was evident that eighty percentage of the signal have a recognition rate of eight and above for some subjects like S4, S6, S11 and S24 and S9 the recognition rates were not appreciable from the analysis were able to conclude that more training data is required to improve the recognition accuracy of events. From the result it was observed that the feasibility of designing a biometric system is possible for some subject using Welch feature for FFNN, while some of the subjects like S4, S6, S11 and S24 and S9 the mean accuracy of four tasks biometric systems was around 75%. Hence, more training was required.

Table 5.18 MUSIC Feature using FFNN Model

	Event			Non -Event	
Tasks / Subjects	Read	Maths	Spell	Relax	Unknown
S1	8	7	9	7	9
S2	6	10	8	7	9
S3	8	8	8	7	9
S4	6	7	9	6	12
S5	7	8	9	8	8
S6	7	9	10	6	8
S7	6	6	7	9	12
S8	8	7	9	9	7
S9	6	7	9	9	9
S10	6	8	9	8	11
S11	7	9	6	7	8
S12	9	8	8	7	7
S13	8	8	9	8	7
S14	7	9	10	7	7
S15	8	7	9	9	8
S16	9	9	8	6	7
S17	8	8	9	8	10
S18	8	8	7	7	11
S19	6	6	9	8	10
S20	7	7	8	8	11
S21	6	7	8	8	7
S22	8	9	9	7	13
S23	6	8	7	6	10
S24	6	8	8	8	10
S25	7	7	8	8	10

**SINGLE TRIAL ANALYSIS**.

The performance of the four biometric tasks designed for each subject is verified through a single trial analysis using a FFNN for PSD algorithm using MUSIC features are shown in Table 5.18. It was observed S3, S9, S17,S22, and S25 was high at a mean of 80%, it is evident that eighty percentage of the signal has a recognition rate of eight and above for some subjects like S7, S11, S20, S21and S24 the recognition rates were not appreciable from the analysis were able to conclude more training is required to improve the recognition accuracy of events. From the result, it was observed that the feasibility of designing a biometric system is possible for some subject using MUSIC feature for FFNN, while for some of the subjects like S7, S11, S20, S21 and S24 the mean accuracy of four tasks biometric system was around 75% only. Hence, more training was required.

5.17 SINGLE TRIAL ANALYSIS FOR RNN

Table 5.19 Covariance Feature Using RNN Model

SINGLE TRIAL ANALYSIS					
Tasks \ Subjects	Event			Non -Event	
	Read	Maths	Spell	Relax	Unknown
S1	8	7	9	7	9
S2	9	9	9	9	4
S3	7	7	8	8	10
S4	8	9	9	8	6
S5	7	8	9	8	8
S6	7	9	10	6	8
S7	8	6	8	9	9
S8	9	7	9	9	6
S9	7	7	10	9	7
S10	9	8	9	8	6
S11	8	9	6	7	10
S12	9	7	9	7	8
S13	9	7	8	8	8
S14	8	9	9	7	7
S15	6	7	9	9	9
S16	6	9	7	6	12
S17	9	8	9	8	6
S18	6	8	8	5	13
S19	6	6	9	5	14
S20	6	7	8	6	13
S21	8	7	8	4	11
S22	7	9	9	9	6
S23	6	8	8	9	9
S24	6	8	8	9	9
S25	6	7	8	7	12

The performance of the four biometric tasks designed for each subject was verified through a single trial analysis using a RNN for PSD algorithm using Covariance features are shown in Table 5.19. It was observed that the acceptance rate of S1, S2, S5, S6, S8, S9, S15, S17 and S22 was high at a mean of 90%. It was evident that eighty percentage of the signals have a recognition rate of eight and above for some subjects like S11, S16, S19, S20, S21, and S25 the recognition rates were not appreciable. From the analysis were able to conclude that more training data was required to improve the recognition accuracy of events. From the result it was observed that the feasibility of designing a biometric system is possible for some subject using Covariance feature for RNN, while for some of the subjects like S11, S16, S19, S20, S21, and S25 the mean accuracy of four task biometric systems was around 80%. Hence, more training was required.

Table 5.20 Burg Feature Using RNN Model

SINGLE TRIAL ANALYSIS					
Tasks / Subjects	**Event**			**Non -Event**	
	Read	**Maths**	**Spell**	**Relax**	**Unknown**
S1	9	8	10	7	6
S2	8	9	8	7	8
S3	8	7	8	7	10
S4	8	8	9	6	9
S5	9	9	9	8	5
S6	8	9	10	6	7
S7	7	6	8	9	10
S8	9	7	9	9	6
S9	7	7	9	9	8
S10	9	8	9	8	6
S11	9	9	10	7	6
S12	8	7	9	7	9
S13	9	7	8	8	8
S14	8	9	9	7	7
S15	6	7	9	9	9
S16	6	9	8	6	11
S17	9	8	9	8	6
S18	6	8	10	7	9
S19	6	6	9	8	11
S20	7	7	8	8	11
S21	8	7	8	8	9
S22	7	9	9	7	8
S23	6	8	8	6	12
S24	6	8	10	8	8
S25	7	7	9	8	9

The performance of the four biometric tasks designed for each subject was verified through a single trial analysis using a FFNN for PSD algorithm using Burg features and is shown in Table 5.20. It was observed for S1, S4, S5, S6, S8, S11, S15, S17, S20,S22 and S25 the acceptance rate was high at a mean of 95%. It is evident that eighty percentage of the signal had a recognition rate of eight and above for some subjects like S7, S19, S21 and S23 the recognition rates were not appreciable. From the analysis it was concluded more training was required to improve the recognition accuracy of events. From the result it was observed that the feasibility of designing a biometric system is possible for some subject using Burg feature for RNN, while for some of the subjects like S7, S19, S21 and S23 the mean accuracy of four tasks biometric systems was around 80%. Hence, more training was required.

Table 5.21 Modified Covariance Feature Using RNN Model

	SINGLE TRIAL ANALYSIS				
Tasks / Subjects	Event			Non -Event	
	Read	Maths	Spell	Relax	Unknown
S1	6	7	9	8	10
S2	8	8	9	8	7
S3	8	9	9	9	6
S4	9	8	10	6	7
S5	9	7	9	8	7
S6	8	7	9	6	10
S7	8	9	7	9	7
S8	9	8	9	9	5
S9	8	8	9	9	6
S10	7	7	9	8	9
S11	9	10	8	9	4
S12	6	8	9	9	8
S13	7	8	8	8	9
S14	9	9	10	7	5
S15	6	7	7	9	11
S16	6	8	8	8	10
S17	9	8	10	8	5
S18	6	8	7	9	10
S19	8	9	9	8	6
S20	6	7	8	8	11
S21	8	7	8	8	9
S22	7	9	8	9	7
S23	6	8	7	6	123
S24	6	8	8	8	10
S25	9	8	8	8	7

The performance of the four biometric tasks designed for each subject is verified through a single trial analysis using RNN for PSD algorithm using Modified Covariance features are shown in Table 5.21. From the Table 5.21 it was observed that the acceptance rate of S4, S5, S6, S7, S8, S9, S10, S11, S17, S19, S22 and S25 was high at a mean of 85% it was evident that eighty percentage of the signal have a recognition rate of nine and above for some subjects like S6, S12, S13, S18, S20, S21 and S23 the recognition rates were not appreciable. From the analysis were able to conclude that more training is required to improve the recognition accuracy of events. From the result, it was observed that the feasibility of designing a biometric system is possible for some subject using the Modified Covariance feature for RNN, while for some of the subjects like S6, S12, S13, S18, S20, S21 and S23 the mean accuracy of four tasks biometric systems was around 75%. Hence, more training was required.

Table 5.22 Yule -Walker Feature Using RNN Model

SINGLE TRIAL ANALYSIS					
Tasks / Subjects	Event			Non -Event	
	Read	Maths	Spell	Relax	Unknown
S1	9	9	10	8	4
S2	7	8	7	6	12
S3	9	8	9	7	7
S4	8	9	9	8	6
S5	8	9	9	11	7
S6	6	8	6	7	13
S7	7	9	10	4	10
S8	7	9	8	6	10
S9	9	7	9	9	6
S10	9	8	8	10	6
S11	6	9	8	5	12
S12	6	7	9	5	13
S13	9	7	8	6	10
S14	8	9	10	4	9
S15	6	7	9	9	9
S16	6	9	8	9	8
S17	9	8	10	9	4
S18	6	8	7	7	12
S19	6	6	9	14	11
S20	6	8	8	10	8
S21	8	8	9	5	10
S22	7	9	7	8	9
S23	6	8	7	4	15
S24	6	8	9	6	11
S25	9	8	8	8	8

The performance of the four biometric tasks designed for each subject was verified through a single trial analysis using a RNN for PSD algorithm using Yule Walker features are shown in Table 5.22. It was observed for S1, S3, S4, S5, S9, S10, S15, S16, S17, S19, S20 and S25 the acceptance rate was high at a mean of 80%, it was evident that eighty percentage of the signals have a recognition rate of eight and above for some subjects like S6, S11, S12, S14, S18 and S28 the recognition rates were not appreciable from the analysis were able to conclude more training is required to improve the recognition accuracy of events. From the result, it was observed that the feasibility of designing a biometric system is possible for some subject using Yule-Walker feature for RNN, while some of the subjects like S6, S11, S12, S14, S18 and S28 the mean accuracy of four tasks biometric systems was around 75%. Hence, more training was required.

Table 5.23 Welch Feature Using RNN Model

SINGLE TRIAL ANALYSIS					
Tasks / Subjects	Event			Non -Event	
	Read	Maths	Spell	Relax	Unknown
S1	8	7	9	9	7
S2	9	8	7	6	10
S3	7	8	8	7	10
S4	7	7	9	6	11
S5	6	8	9	8	9
S6	8	9	8	6	9
S7	7	6	7	9	11
S8	8	8	9	9	6
S9	8	7	10	9	6
S10	9	8	9	8	6
S11	8	9	8	7	8
S12	8	8	8	7	9
S13	9	9	9	8	5
S14	8	9	10	7	6
S15	6	7	9	9	9
S16	6	9	8	6	11
S17	9	8	9	8	6
S18	6	8	7	7	12
S19	6	6	9	7	8
S20	6	7	8	9	10
S21	8	7	8	6	11
S22	7	9	10	8	6
S23	6	8	9	7	10
S24	6	8	8	8	11
S25	6	8	8	7	11

The performance of the four biometric tasks designed for each subject was verified through a single trial analysis using a RNN for PSD algorithm using Welch features are shown in Table 5.23. It was observed for S1, S8, S9, S10, S13, S15, S17, S22 and S22 the acceptance rate was high at a mean of 80%, it is evident that eighty percentage of the signal had a recognition rate of eight and above for some subjects like S7, S21 and S23 the recognition rates were not appreciable from the analysis were able to conclude that more training data is required to improve the recognition accuracy of events. From the result, it was observed that the feasibility of designing a biometric system is possible for some subject using Welch feature for RNN, while for some of the subjects like S7, S21 and S23 the mean accuracy of four tasks biometric systems was around 75%. Hence, more training was required.

Table 5.24 Multiple Signal Classification Feature Using RNN Model

SINGLE TRIAL ANALYSIS					
	Event			Non -Event	
Tasks / Subjects	Read	Maths	Spell	Relax	Unknown
S1	9	8	9	6	8
S2	8	9	8	4	9
S3	8	10	8	7	7
S4	8	7	9	6	10
S5	9	8	9	5	9
S6	9	9	10	6	6
S7	9	6	8	9	8
S8	10	7	9	9	5
S9	10	7	9	9	5
S10	6	8	9	8	9
S11	7	9	10	6	8
S12	9	7	9	7	8
S13	9	7	9	8	7
S14	8	9	8	7	8
S15	8	7	9	6	10
S16	7	7	7	6	13
S17	9	8	10	8	5
S18	6	8	7	7	12
S19	6	6	9	7	12
S20	6	8	8	7	11
S21	8	8	8	8	8
S22	7	7	8	7	11
S23	6	8	7	6	13
S24	6	8	8	6	12
S25	7	8	8	7	10

The performance of the four biometric tasks designed for each subject was verified through a single trial analysis using a FFNN for PSD algorithm using MUSIC features are shown in Table 5.24. It was observed the acceptance rate of S1, S3, S6, S8, S9, S15 and S17 and S25 was high at a mean of 85% it is evident that eighty percentage of the signal have a recognition rate of eight and above for some subjects like S2, S18, S19, S20 and S23 the recognition rates were not appreciable. From the analysis were able to conclude that more training is required to improve the recognition accuracy of events. From the result, it was observed that the feasibility of designing a biometric system is possible for some subject using the MUSIC feature for RNN, while for some of the subjects like S2, S18, S19, S20 and S23 the mean accuracy of four task biometric systems was around 75%. Hence, more training was required.

5.18 PREDICTIVE POWER ANALYSIS

Four measures are often used to measure the accuracy and predictive power of a BMI. They are specificity, true positive also known as sensitivity, false positive rate and accuracy. Let TP be true positive values which are true detection of individuals, FN be false negative values which remain undetected; FP be false positive values which are false detected event; TN be true negative. Which are classified as non event, P be the total number of positive cases and N be the total number of negative cases. Sensitivity and specificity are statistical measures of a performance of a sample classification test. Sensitivity measures the proportion of actual positives which is the total number of correctly identified subjects. Specificity measures the proportion of negatives which are correctly identified (Hudson et al., 2000). The performance of the classifier is also assessed in terms of sensitivity and specificity is as follows:

$$\text{Specificity} = TN/N \tag{6.1}$$

$$\text{True Positive Rate (sensitivity)} = TP / (TP+FN) \tag{6.2}$$

$$\text{False positive rate} = FP /(TN+FP) \tag{6.3}$$

$$\text{Accuracy} = (TP+TN) /(P+N) \tag{6.4}$$

$$\text{Positive} = (TP+FP) \tag{6.5}$$

$$\text{Negative} = (TN+FN) \tag{6.6}$$

The TP, TN, FP and FN values are derived from Single trial (sample by sample) experiment results performed on FFNN and RNN for PSD features. The predictive power analysis results for both events and nonevents using Power Spectral Density features are shown in Table 5.13 to 5.24. It was observed that the spell task has better specificity, sensitivity and accuracy rate compared with the remaining task using FFNN and RNN. The results show that the RNN models are more suitable for classifying the EEG signal for four tasks using PSD features. From the results obtained it was observed that the performance of RNN model using Burg features is higher when compared to the FFNN models.

5.19 EVALUATION OF CUSTOMIZED BMI USING BIT TRANSFER RATE

The BMI performance can also be evaluated using the bit transfer rate. The bit transfer rate is defined as the amount of information communicated per unit of time. This parameter encompasses speed and accuracy in a signal value. The bit rate can be used for comparing the different BMI approaches and for the measurement of system improvements (Dornhege et al., 2006). The bit transfer rate for four tasks by using Power Spectral Density features are shown in Table 5.25 to 5.36. The bit transfer rate is calculated from equation 6.7.

$$\text{Bit transfer rate} = \frac{60}{T_{act}}\left[\log_2 n + p_a \log_2 p_a + (1 - p_a) \log_2 \frac{1 - p_a}{n - 1}\right] \qquad (6.7)$$

N = number of task

P_a = mean Accuracy

1-P_a = mean recognition error

T $_{act}$ = Action period (in Seconds) can be proposed by (Wolpaw, 1988).

Table 5.25 Bit Transfer Rate of FFNN Using Covariance Feature

Tasks	TP	TN	FP	FN	SEN	SPE	FPR	ACC	BTR
Read	84	82	22	12	0.87	0.88	0.21	0.83	6.4
Relax	82	80	23	15	0.84	0.85	0.22	0.81	6.27
Maths	82	80	24	14	0.85	0.85	0.23	0.81	6.2
Spell	86	82	21	11	0.88	0.89	0.2	0.84	6.43

The performance accuracy of the BMI was evaluated using the bit transfer rate. The result of the bit transfer rate for four biometric tasks was found using FFNN with Covariance algorithm are shown in Table 5.25. It is observed that the FFNN has a mean accuracy 84% for the read task for Covariance algorithm. The bit rate for the FFNN of 6.43 is obtained for spell task with samples from two sessions of ten trials each. The sensitivity verifying the individuals through EEG signals are validated.

Table 5.26 Bit Transfer Rate of FFNN Using Burg Feature

Tasks	TP	TN	FP	FN	SEN	SPE	FPR	ACC	BTR
Read	82	80	26	12	0.87	0.87	0.25	0.81	6.2
Relax	80	79	24	17	0.82	0.82	0.23	0.80	6.12
Maths	81	80	29	10	0.89	0.89	0.27	0.81	6.21
Spell	84	81	24	11	0.88	0.88	0.23	0.81	6.27

The performance accuracy of the BMI was evaluated using bit transfer rate. The results of the bit transfer rate for four biometric tasks using FFNN with Burg algorithm is shown in Table 5.26. It is observed that the FFNN has a mean accuracy of 81% for the read, spell and maths task. For Burg algorithm the bit rate for FFNN of 6.27 was obtained for spell task with samples from two sessions of ten trials each. The sensitivity of verifying the individuals through EEG signals are validated.

Table 5.27 Bit Transfer Rate of FFNN Using Modified Covariance Feature

Tasks	TP	TN	FP	FN	SEN	SPE	FPR	ACC	BTR
Read	82	79	25	14	0.85	0.85	0.24	0.81	6.27
Relax	80	79	24	17	0.82	0.82	0.23	0.80	6.12
Maths	80	78	20	13	0.86	0.86	0.27	0.79	6.04
Spell	84	80	24	12	0.87	0.88	0.23	0.82	6.27

The performance accuracy of the BMI was evaluated using bit transfer rate. The results of the bit transfer rate for four biometric tasks using FFNN with Modified Covariance algorithm are shown in Table 5.27. It is observed that the FFNN has a mean accuracy of 82% for the spell task for Modified Covariance algorithm the bit rate for FFNN of 6.27 was obtained for read and spell task with samples from two sessions of ten trials each. The sensitivity of verifying the individuals through EEG signals are validated.

Table 5.28 Bit Transfer Rate of FFNN Using Yule Walker Feature

Task	TP	TN	FP	FN	SEN	SPE	FPR	ACC	BTR
Read	81	81	23	15	0.84	0.84	0.22	0.81	6.2
Relax	80	79	24	17	0.82	0.82	0.23	0.80	6.12
Maths	80	79	26	15	0.84	0.82	0.25	0.80	6.12
Spell	83	81	22	14	0.85	0.86	0.21	0.82	6.27

The performance accuracy of the BMI was evaluated using the bit transfer rate. The results of the bit transfer rate for four biometric task using FFNN with Yule Walker algorithm shown in Table 5.28. It is observed that the FFNN has a mean accuracy of 82% for the spell task. Yule Walker algorithm the bit rate for the FFNN of 6.27 is obtained for spell task with samples from two sessions of ten trials. The sensitivity verifying the individuals through EEG signals are validated

Table 5.29 Bit Transfer Rate of FFNN Using Welch Feature

Tasks	TP	TN	FP	FN	SEN	SPE	FPR	ACC	BTR
Read	81	81	23	15	0.84	0.84	0.22	0.81	6.2
Relax	80	79	24	17	0.82	0.82	0.23	0.80	6.12
Maths	80	79	26	15	0.84	0.82	0.25	0.80	6.12
Spell	83	81	22	14	0.85	0.86	0.21	0.82	6.27

The performance accuracy of the BMI was evaluated using bit transfer rate. The results of the bit transfer rate for four biometric tasks using FFNN with Welch algorithm are shown in Table 5.29. It is observed that the FFNN has a mean accuracy 82% of the spell task for Welch algorithm the bit rate for the FFNN of 6.27 was obtained for spell task with samples from two sessions of ten trials. The sensitivity verifying the individuals through EEG signals are validated.

Table 5.30 Bit Transfer Rate of FFNN Using MUSIC Feature

Tasks	TP	TN	FP	FN	SEN	SPE	FPR	ACC	BTR
Read	80	74	27	19	0.85	0.83	0.22	0.79	6.04
Relax	80	79	24	17	0.82	0.82	0.23	0.80	6.12
Maths	80	73	32	25	0.85	0.83	0.22	0.79	6.04
Spell	82	85	28	15	0.86	0.84	0.22	0.81	6.11

The performance accuracy of the BMI was evaluated using bit transfer rate. The results of the bit transfer rate for four biometric tasks using FFNN with MUSIC algorithm shown in Table 5.30. It is observed that the FFNN has a mean accuracy of 81% for the spell task for MUSIC algorithm the bit rate for FFNN of 6.12 was obtained for relax task with samples from two sessions of ten trials each. The sensitivity verifying the individuals through EEG signals are validated.

Table 5.31 Bit Transfer Rate of RNN Using Covariance Feature

Tasks	TP	TN	FP	FN	SEN	SPE	FPR	ACC	BTR
Read	82	80	25	13	0.86	0.86	0.24	0.81	6.2
Relax	80	79	24	17	0.82	0.82	0.23	0.80	6.12
Maths	80	79	27	14	0.85	0.85	0.25	0.80	6.12
Spell	83	81	24	12	0.87	0.87	0.23	0.82	6.27

The performance accuracy of the BMI was evaluated using the bit transfer rate. The results of the bit transfer rate for four biometric task using RNN with Covariance algorithm shown in Table 5.31. It was observed that the RNN has a mean accuracy of 82% for the spell task for Covariance algorithm the bit rate for the RNN of 6.27 was obtained for spell task with samples from two sessions of ten trials. The sensitivity verifying the individuals through the EEG signals are validated.

Table 5.32 Bit Transfer Rate of RNN Using Burg Feature

Tasks	TP	TN	FP	FN	SEN	SPE	FPR	ACC	BTR
Read	80	74	27	19	0.85	0.83	0.22	0.79	6.04
Relax	80	73	32	25	0.85	0.83	0.22	0.79	6.04
Maths	80	79	24	17	0.82	0.82	0.23	0.80	6.12
Spell	82	85	28	15	0.85	0.86	0.24	0.83	6.57

The performance accuracy of the BMI was evaluated using the bit transfer rate. The results of the bit transfer rate for four biometric task using RNN with Burg algorithm shown in Table 5.32. It was observed that the Burg has a mean accuracy of 83% for spell task for Burg algorithm, the bit rate for the Burg of 6.12 was obtained for relax and maths tasks with samples from two sessions of ten trials. The results are obtained and validate the feasibility of verifying the individuals through EEG signal.

Table 5.33 Bit Transfer Rate of RNN Using Modified Covariance Feature

Tasks	TP	TN	FP	FN	SEN	SPE	FPR	ACC	BTR
Read	80	74	27	19	0.85	0.83	0.22	0.79	6.04
Relax	80	79	24	17	0.82	0.82	0.23	0.80	6.12
Maths	80	73	32	25	0.85	0.83	0.22	0.79	6.04
Spell	82	85	28	15	0.86	0.84	0.22	0.81	6.11

The performance accuracy of the BMI was evaluated using the bit transfer rate. The results of the bit transfer rate for four biometric tasks using RNN with Modified Covariance Feature algorithm shown in Table 5.33. It was observed that the RNN has a mean accuracy of 81% of the spell task for Modified Covariance algorithm the bit rate for the RNN of 6.12 was obtained for relax task with samples from two sessions of ten trials. The results are obtained and validate the feasibility of verifying the individuals through EEG signal.

Table 5.34 Bit Transfer Rate of RNN Using Yule-walker Feature

Task	TP	TN	FP	FN	SEN	SPE	FPR	ACC	BTR
Read	80	77	25	18	0.85	0.83	0.22	0.78	6.06
Relax	80	79	24	17	0.82	0.82	0.23	0.80	6.12
Maths	80	78	26	16	0.84	0.82	0,25	0.80	6.12
Spell	82	79	24	15	0.84	0.82	0,24	0.79	6.08

The performance accuracy of the BMI was evaluated using the bit transfer rate. The results of the bit transfer rate for four biometric tasks using RNN with Yule-walker algorithm shown in Table 5.34. It was observed that the RNN has a mean accuracy of 80% of the relax and maths tasks for Covariance algorithm the bit rate for the RNN of 6.12 was obtained for relax and maths tasks with samples from two sessions of ten trials. The results are obtained and validate the feasibility of verifying the individuals through EEG signal.

Table 5.35 Bit Transfer Rate of RNN Using Welch Feature

Task	TP	TN	FP	FN	SEN	SPE	FPR	ACC	BTR
Read	81	75	28	16	0.84	0.81	0.22	0.78	6.5
Relax	80	79	24	17	0.82	0.82	0.23	0.80	6.02
Maths	80	79	25	16	0.85	0.82	0.21	0.76	6.02
Spell	82	78	29	12	0.85	0.84	0.21	0.80	6.12

The performance accuracy of the BMI was evaluated using the bit transfer rate. The results of the bit transfer rate for four biometric task using RNN with Welch algorithm shown in Table 5.35. It was observed that the RNN has a mean accuracy of 80% for the relax and spell task for Welch algorithm the bit rate for the RNN of 6.12 was obtained for spell task with samples from two sessions of ten trials. The results are obtained and validate the feasibility of verifying the individuals through EEG signal.

Table 5.36 Bit Transfer Rate of RNN Using MUSIC Feature

Tasks	TP	TN	FP	FN	SEN	SPE	FPR	ACC	BTR
Read	80	77	25	18	0.85	0.83	0.22	0.78	6.06
Relax	80	79	24	17	0.82	0.82	0.23	0.80	6.12
Maths	80	78	26	16	0.84	0.82	0.25	0.80	6.12
Spell	82	79	24	15	0.84	0.82	0.24	0.79	6.08

The performance accuracy of the BMI was evaluated using the bit transfer rate. The results of the bit transfer rate for four biometric tasks using RNN with MUSIC algorithm shown in Table 5.36. It was observed that the RNN has a mean accuracy of 80% of the relax and maths task for MUSIC algorithm the bit rate for the RNN of 6.12 was obtained for relax and maths tasks with samples from two sessions of ten trials. The results are obtained and validate the feasibility of verifying the individuals through EEG signal.

5.20 SUMMARY

The results are analyzed using single channel and two channel system. Two network and six feature extraction algorithms are used in these channels. In single channel, Covariance, Burg, Covariance, Modified Covariance, Welch, MUSIC and Yule Walker in two channels Covariance, Burg, Modified Covariance, Welch, MUSIC and Yule Walker these feature are used. Comparing both single channel and two channel system Burg algorithm spell task had got higher accuracy of spell task. Two channel systems had got higher amount of accuracy. So single trial analysis and bit transfer rate was analyzed by two channel system.

CHAPTER 6

CONCLUSION AND FUTURE WORK

This chapter presents an overview of the thesis, summarizes its key contributions and discusses their implication on the biometric authentication system. It also presents the opportunities for further research in this area.

6.1 SUMMARY OF THE RESEARCH WORK

The works discussed in this research EEG based biometric authentication system using brain signature, which is a part of a biometric security system. A biometric system is used in two different modes they are authentication and identification. Identity authentication occurs when the user claimed to be already enrolled in the system;in this case the biometric data obtained from the user are compared to the user data already stored in the database. Identification occurs when the user biometric data is matched against all the records in the database as the user can be anywhere in the database or he/she actually does not have to be there at all. The biometric recognition or biometrics refers to the automatic authentication of a person based on his / her physiological (e.g., fingerprint, iris) or behavioral (e.g., signature) characteristics or traits. Biometric techniques can potentially prevent unauthorized access to ATMs, cellular phones, laptops, and computer networks.

There are also many drawbacks in biometric systems and one of the drawbacks is spoof attacks. In this an impostor may attempt to spoof the biometric trait of a legitimate enrolled user in order to circumvent the system. This type of attack is especially relevant to biometric systems. For face recognition system data acquisition is difficult, the user must face in the same position each access, background lighting important for accurate verification. In fingerprint recognition the drawbacks are in rare situations like people without fingers. In biometric applications, there are many drawbacks. Hence I have chosen EEG brain signature. EEG brain signals have a unique brain wave pattern, which cannot be imposters. EEG as a biometric is relatively new compared to other biometrics. The proposed biometric system has several advantages :(a) It is confidential (as it corresponds to a biometric tasks) (b) It is difficult to mimic (as a similar mental task are person dependent) (c) It is almost impossible to steal (as brain activity is sensitive to the stress and the mood of the person to produce his / her mental pass-phrase).

In this research four protocols are designed using brain signals. The EEG brain signature of an individual is verified using neural network. The EEG signals are taken on the basis of 10-20 electrode placement system. The standard 10-20 electrode placement measurement is followed for recording the EEG brain signals. Signals were collected from 50 subject's in a single channel system with the subject their age is between 18-45 years. Three non invasive electrodes which are gold plated cup shaped disks placed at FP1, F4 and O2. The subjects were seated comfortably in a noise free room. The subjects did not make any overt movement and were requested to perform four biometric tasks, namely read, relax, maths and spell. The EEG signals were recorded for 10 sec during the task. The data were collected for two sessions on different days. The sampling frequency was fixed at 200 Hz. In a single channel system feature extraction techniques, namely PSD with parametric, non parametric and high resolution method are used. Parametric methods such as Burg method, Covariance method, Modified Covariance and Yule- Walker methods are used. The techniques behind these methods are discussed briefly. In the non-parametric method the Welch method is used. For high resolution method MUSIC is used. In the classification process, two network models, namely FFNN and RNN are used for the classification of EEG brain signals. The minimum classification accuracy of FFNN was 81.1% for math task using MUSIC algorithm and the maximum classification accuracy for spell task was 95% for RNN using the Burg algorithm.

Fifty subjects were performed in single channel system. From the 50 subjects 25 subjects were selected to perform the two channel systems with their age between 18-45 years. Five non invasive electrodes were used in this experiment. The electrodes are gold plated cup shaped disks placed at FP1, F3, F4, O1 and O2. The subjects were seated comfortably in a noise free room. The subject did not make any overt movement and requested to perform four biometric tasks, namely read, relax, maths and spell. The EEG signals were recorded for 10 sec during the task. The data were collected for two sessions on different days. The sampling frequency was fixed at 200 Hz. The feature extraction and classification algorithm which are used in a single channel system are used in a two channel system. The minimum classification accuracy of FFNN was 86% for relax task using a Yule – walker algorithm and the maximum classification accuracy for spell task was 98.05% for RNN using the Burg algorithm.

While comparing the single channel system with the two channel system have better results, hence the single trial analysis was found for two channel system. In a single trial analysis of burg feature using FFNN the subjects which have high authentication rate are S1, S2, S5, S9, S13, S15, S17, S19 and S22. In a single trial analysis of burg feature using RNN the subjects which have high authentication rate are S1, S2, S16, S17, S18, S22 and S25. A graphical user interface GUI was developed to test the biometric system development. The GUI performed classification rates from 70% to 95%. Comparing of the entire task, the spell task gave the highest pattern authentication. Result validate that two channel acquisitions prove gives a marginally better recognition rate for person authentication. Experiments conducted on the 98 network models show that the RNN has the best performance rate than FFNN. Among the four biometric tasks proposed in the study, the spell task has outperformed the other three tasks and hence is found to be more suitable for biometric authentication. Better algorithm is to be developed to improve the recognition tasks which will be the focus of our future studies.

6.1.1 Contributions 1

The EEG protocols are designed. Then the EEG signal are collected for 50 subjects using single channel system and 25 subjects for two channel system respectively.

6.1.2 Contribution 2

The raw EEG signals are used to extract the prominent features. These features are used in pattern verification.

6.1.3 Contribution 3

Design and development of a Graphical User Interface (GUI) for biometric authentication using brain signature.

6.2 COMMERCIALIZATION POTENTIAL

This product has a very good commercial potential. It can be used in high security level with limited people accessing to it. Existing biometrics have a lot of drawbacks and has doubts how secured it is. Since, it has proven that brain signature has modality of confidential, difficult to mimic and impossible to steal. It is suitable to be used in this modern era because the crime rate is increasing and threatening the human being.

6.3 FUTURE WORK

1. Investigate the proposed techniques for scalability.
2. Authentication is another major growing concern; this aspect of EEG brain signature is to be further investigated.
3. Online real time studies to be conducted based on spell task to evaluate the algorithm for real time application which will also be proposed in our future work.

REFERENCE

Aggarwal G., N.K Ratha, J.Tsai-Yang and R.M Bolle, 2008. Gradient Based Textural Characterization of Fingerprints. In proceedings of IEEE International conference on Biometrics: Theory, Applications and Systems.

Akankshya Shradhanjali, Subhra Chowdhury and Neelesh Kumar, 2013. Power Spectral Density Estimation of EMG Signals Using Parametric and Non-Parametric Approach. 2(4):111-117.

Akhtar, Muhammad Tahir, Mitsuhashi, Wataru and James, J.Christopher, 2012. Employing Spatially Constrained ICA and Wavelet Denoising, for Automatic Removal of Artifacts from Multichannel EEG Data. Signal Processing. 92(2): 401-416.

Alessandra A. Paulino, Student Member, 2013. Latent Fingerprint Matching Using Descriptor-Based Hough Transform, Vol. 8(1).

Anil K. Jain, Kai Cao, S. Sunpreet, Arora, 2014. Recognizing Infants and Toddlers Using Fingerprints: Increasing the Vaccination Coverage: 1-8.

Anil K. Jain, 2004. An Introduction to Biometric Recognition. Vol.14(1).

Babiloni F,C. Baibiloni,F.carducci,M.del Gaudio and P.onorati and A.Urbano., 1997a. A High Resolution Method Based On The Correction of The Surface Laplacian Estimate For The Subject Varible Of The Scalp Thickness.103(4):486-492.

Bishop C.M., 1995. Neural Networks for Pattern Recognition. Oxford: Clarendon Press.

Blanco, 1995. Time-Frequency Analysis of Electroencephalogram series: 51 (3).

Bronzino J. D., 1995. Principles of Electroencephalography. The Biomedical Engineering Handbook: 201-212.

Bronzino J.D, 2000. Regulation of the Medical Device Innovation. The Biomedical Engineering Handbook.

Cempirek M, J.Stastny, 2007. The Optimization of the EEG-Based Biometric Classification. Applied Electronics: 25-28.

Chellappa R., C.L Wilson and C.Sirohey , 1995. Human and Machine Recognition of Faces: A Survey. Proc. IEEE, 83(5): 705-740.

Chen Y., S.C Dass and A.K Jain, 2006. Localized Iris Image Quality Using 2-D Wavelets. IEEE International Conference on Biometrics.

ChinTeng Lin, ShengFu Liang, YuChien Chen, YungChi Hsu, and LiWei Ko, 2006. Driver's Drowsiness Estimation by Combining EEG Signal Analysis and ICAbased Fuzzy Neural Networks. IEEE Int. Symp. On Circuits and Systems: 2125 - 2128.

Collura T., 1998. A Guide to Electrode Selection, Location and Application for EEG.

Dai J., J. Feng, J. Zhou, 2012. Robust and Efficient Ridge-Based Palm Print Matching. IEEE Transaction on Pattern Analysis and Machine Intelligence, Vol.34 (8): 0162-8828.

Daugman J., 2005. Recognizing Persons By Their Iris Patterns, In Biometrics: Personal Identification In A Networked Society. 103–121.

Delorme A, T. Jung, T. Sejnowski, and S. Makeig, 2007. Improved Rejection of Artifacts From EEG Data Using High-Order Statistics And Independent Component Analysis. Neuroimage: 1443–1449.

Dhaparidze KO, AM.Yaglom, 1983. Spectrum Parameter Estimation in Time Series Analysis. 4(1):1–96

Djuric PM and Kay SM, 1999. Spectral Estimation and Modeling.

Edlinger G, P.Wach, G. Pfurtscheller, 1988. On The Realization of an Analytic High Resolutioneeg.736-745.

Fisch and Spehlmann, 1999. EEG Primer: Basic Principles of Digital and Analog EEG.

Flom L and S. Aran, 1987. Iris Recognition System. U.S. Patent.

Gerwin Schalk., 2004. A General-Purpose Brain-Computer Interface (BCI) System. IEEE Transactions on Biomedical Engineering, 51(6).

Gevins A.S, P.Brickett, BCostales, J,Le and B.Reutter, 1990. Beyond Topographic Mapping Towards Functional Anatomical Imaging with 124 Channels EEG and 3-D MRI.53-64

Ghandeharion H and H.Ahmadi-Noubari, 2009. Detection dnd Removal Of Ocular Artifacts Using Independent Component Analysis And Wavelets. Paper Presented At The Neural Engineering.

Hass S.H, M.G Frei, I. Osorio, B. Pasik-Duncan and J. Radel, 2003. EEG Ocular Artifact Removal through ARMAX Model System Identification Using Extended Least Squares, Communication in Formation and System.3 (1): 19- 40.

Hayes M.H, 1996. Statistical Digital Signal Processing and Modeling.

Hebert M., 2008. Text-Dependent Speaker Recognition. In Springer Handbook Of Speech Processing: 743–762.

Hema C. R, M. P. Paulraj, S. Yaacob, A. H. Adom, and R. Nagarajan, 2008. Functional Link PSO Neural Network Based Classification of EEG Mental Task Signals. IEEE.Vol(3):1-6.

Hema C.R, ,Paulraj M.P, Harkirenjit Kaur.,2008. Brain signature : A Modality For Biometric Authentication. IEEE:1-4

Huang W and D. Zhang, 2008. Palm Print Verification Based on Robust Line Orientation Code: 1504 – 1513

Jain A K., R. Bolle, and S. Pankanti, 1999. Biometrics: Personal Identification in Networked Society.

Jain A. K., S. Prabhkar, L Hong and S. Pankanti., 2000. Filter Bank Based Fingerprint Matching. IEEE Transactions on Image Processing. (9): 846-853.

Jain A. K., A. Ross and S. Prabhkar S., 2004. An Introduction to Biometric Recognition. Vol. 14: 4-20.

Jasper H.H., 1958. The Ten-Twenty Electrode System of the International Federation. Electroencephalography and Clinical Neurophysiology: 371-375.

Jhat Z. A., A.H Mir and S. Rubab., 2011. Fingerprint Texture Feature for Discrimination and Personal Verification. International Journal of Security and its Applications: 5(3).

Karungaru S, M. Fukumi, M. Akamatsu., 2004. Feature Extraction for Face Detuction and Recognition. IEEE International Workshop on Robot and Human Interactive Communication.Vol (1):235-239.

Katharine Brigham and B. V. K. Vijaya Kumar., 2010. Subject Identification from Electroencephalogram (EEG) Signals During Imagined Speech. IEEE.

Kay S. M, 1988. Modern Spectral Estimation Theory and Application.

Keith AW, FW Robert, FI Michael and JH Timothy., 1993. Application of AR Spectral Analysis to Cepstral Estimation of Mean Scatterer Spacing. IEEE transactions on Ultrasonics, Ferroelectrics and Frequency Control. 40(1):51- 58.

Kirby R.S, Withington, A.B Darling, F.G Kilgour., 1990. Engineering in History, New York, Dover Publication.

Kong A., D. Zhang and G.M Lu., 2006. A Study of Identical Twin's Palm Prints for Personal Verification. Pattern Recognition. 39 (11): 2149–2156.

Lawrence.S,1987. Digital Spectral Analysis.

Manzoor Khazi , Atul Kumar and M. J Vidya., 2012. Analysis of EEG Using 10:20 Electrode System. International Journal of Innovative Research in Science, Engineering and Technology 1(2).

Millett, David, 2001. Hans Berger: From Psychic Energy to the EEG. Volume 44(4): 522-542.

Miltner W H., C. Braun, M. Arnold, H. Witte and E. Taub., 1999. Coherence of Gamma-Band EEG Activity as A Basis For Associative Learning: 434 –436.

Mohamed sotane, 2010. Product of Likelihood Ratio Scores Fusion of Dynamic Face and On-line Signature Based Biometrics Verification International Journal of Database Theory and Application Vol.8 (4): 91-106

Muhammad Kamil Abdullah, Khazaimatol S. Subari, Justin Leo Cheang Loong and Nurul Nadia Ahmad, 2010. Analysis of the EEG Signal for a Practical Biometric System. International Journal of Medical, Health, Biomedical, Bioengineering and Pharmaceutical Engineering: 4(8).

Niedermeyer E, 1999. EEG Bands: A Computer Program to Statistically Analyze Parameters of Electroencephalographic Signals: 4(7).

Niedermeyer E., F. H. Lopes da Silva, 1993. Electroencephalography: Basic Principles, Clinical Applications and Related Field.

Nunez P.L., 1995. Neocortical Dynamics and Human EEG Rhythms.

Nuria Masso, Ferran Rey, Dani Romero, Gabriel Gual, Lluís Costa and Ana German, 2010. Surface Electromyography Applications in the Sport. 45(165):121-130.

Osamah Al, Hamdani, Ali Chekima, Jamal Dargham, Sh-Hussain Salleh, Fuad Noman and Hadri Hussain, 2003. Multimodal Biometrics Based on Identification and Verification System.

Palaniappan.R. Two-stage biometric authentication method using thought activity brain waves. Int'l J. Neural Systems, 18(01):59–66, 2008.

Paranjape R, J. Mahovsky, L. Benedicenti and Z. Koles, 2001. The Electroencephalogram as a Biometric. In Canadian Conference on Electrical and Computer Engineering, (2): 1363 –1366.

Park H.J, D. Jeong and K.S Park, 2002. Automated Detection and Elimination of Periodic ECG Artifacts in EEG Using the Energy Interval Histogram Method. 49(12):1526-1533.

Poulos, M. Rangoussi N. Alexandris and A. Evangelou, 2001. On the use of EEG Features towards Person Identification via Neural Networks. Informatics for Health and Social Care, 261: 35-48.

Prasad S.M., V. K. Govindan and P. S. Sathidevi, 2009. Palm Print Authentication Using Fusion of Wavelet Based Representations.

Proakis J.G and.G Manolakis, 1996. Digital Signal Processing Principles Algorithms and Applications.

Rafik Djemili., Mouldi Bedda and Hocine Bourouba, 2007. A Hybrid GMM/SVM System for Text Independent Speaker Identification. International Journal of Electrical, Computer, Energetic, Electronic and Communication Engineering, 1(4).

Ramaswamy Palaniappan., 2006. Multiple Mental Thought Parametric Classification: A New Approach for Individual Identification. Proceeding of International Journal of Signal Processing, Volume (2):222-226.

Ravi K and R. Palaniappan, 2005. Leave-One-Out Authentication of Persons Using 40Hz EEG Oscillations. In The International Conference on Computer as a Tool (2): 1386 – 1389.

Ravi K V R and R. Palaniappan, 2005. Recognizing Individuals Using Their Brain Patterns. In Proceedings of the Third International Conference on Information Technology and Applications, vol. 2: 520 – 523.

Ridderinkhof K. R., S.Nieuwenhuis and T.R Bashore, 2003. Errors Are Foreshadowed In Brain Potentials Associated With Action Monitoring In Cingulate Cortex In Humans.

Riera A, A. Soria-Frisch, M. Caparrini, C. Grau and G. Ruffini., 2008. Unobtrusive Biometric System Based on Electroencephalogram Analysis. EURASIP Journal on Advances in Signal Processing.

Sabarigiri B and D. Suganyadevi, 2014. An Efficient Multimodal Biometric Authentication based on IRIS and Electroencephalogram (EEG).

Sadasivan, P.K and Narayana D, 1995. Line Interference Cancellation From Corrupted EEG Signals Using Modified Linear Phase FIR Digital Filters: 3.35-3.36.

Sanei S. and J. Chambers, 2007. EEG Signal Processing.

Schmid N., M. Ketkar, H. Singh, and B. Cukic, 2006. Performance Analysis of Iris-Based Identification System at the Matching Score Level. IEEE Transactions on Information Forensics and Security. 1(2):154–168.

Senthil Kumar P, R. Arumuganathan, K. Sivakumar and C. Vimal, 2009 . An Adaptive method to remove ocular artifacts from EEG signals using Wavelet Transform. Journal of Applied Sciences Research, 5(7): 741-745.

Shiliang Sun., 2008. Multitask Learning for EEG-Based Biometrics. Proceeding of International Conference on Patter Recognition: 51-55.

Shu W and D. Zhang, 1998. Automated Personal Identification by Palm Print. Optical Engineering, 37(8): 2359-2362.

Sivanandam S.N, Paulraj M., 2003. Introduction to Artificial Neural Networks.

Sonia sangwanet, 2015. A Review on: Iris Recognition. International Journal of Computer Science and Information Technologies, Vol. 6 (4): 3871-3873.

Sornmo L and P. Laguna, 2005. Bioelectrical Signal Processing in Cardiac and Neurological Applications.

Soyuj Kumar Sahoo and S R Mahadeva Prasanna. Bimodal Biometric Person AuthenticationUsing Speech and Face Under Degraded Condition.

Sravya.K, S. Rajeswari, K.V.Ramana Murthy., 2012. Design and Evaluation Of Time Dependent Oral Colon Targeted Drug Delivery Systems For Tinidazole Using Eudragit. Vol.3 (1): 564-575.

Srinivasan. R., D.M Tucker and M. Murias., 1998. Estimating the Spatial Nyquist of The Human EEG, Behavior Research Methods: 8-19.

Subha D.P, P.K Joseph, A.U Rajendra and C.M Lim, 2010. EEG Signal Analysis: A Survey. 34:195-212.

Teplan, M, 2002. Fundamentals of EEG Measurement. Measurement Science Review, Vol 2(2).

Tyner F. S, J. R.Knott., 1989. Fundamentals of EEG Technology, Vol 1.

Vijay Khare, Jayashree Santhosh, Sneh Anand, Manvir Bhatia., 2010. Classification of Five Mental Tasks Based on Two Methods of Neural Network. (IJCSIS) International Journal of Computer Science and Information Security: 8(3).

Wang Y.L, J.H Liu and Y.C Liu., 2008. Automatic Removal of Ocular Artifacts from Electroencephalogram Using Hilbert Huang Transform: 2138 – 2141.

Wenjie Xu and S. Cuntai Guan Ranganatha., 2004. High Accuracy Classification of EEG Signal, (2).

Woodward J.D., N. M. Orlands and P. T. Higgins., 2003. Biometrics: Identity Assurance In the Information Age. McGraw-Hill, Osborne, Berkeley, California, USA.

Yasrebi S SH and M. Emamim., 2008. Application of Artificial Neural Networks (ANNs) in Prediction and Interpretation of Pressure Meter Test Results. International Conference of International Association for Computer Methods and Advances in Geomechanics (IACMAG).

Zhang L and D. Zhang., 2004. Characterization of Palm Prints by Wavelet Signatures via directional Context modeling. IEEE: 34 (3): 1335–1347.

www.ingramcontent.com/pod-product-compliance
Lightning Source LLC
Chambersburg PA
CBHW080903160726
48000CB00009B/2841